TIβETAN

MAGIC

—✦— AND —✦—

MYSTICISM

About the Author

J. H. (Herbie) Brennan is an acclaimed author of seventy books of fiction and nonfiction, several of which have become international bestsellers. His works have appeared in more than fifty countries of Europe, Asia, North and South America, and Australia. His *Grailquest* series of adventure game-books for young readers is a phenomenal success worldwide.

Brennan started his intellectual journey at an early age, studying psychology virtually from the time he could read, and hypnotizing a school friend at age nine! At twenty-four, he was the youngest newspaper editor in his native Ireland. By his midtwenties, he had published his first novel, and his out-of-body experience work *Astral Doorways* is a classic in its field.

Herbie Brennan is a man of ideas. In addition to his work as an author, he maintains an active interest in software development, self-improvement techniques, and reincarnation research. He is a frequent lecturer and media guest throughout the United Kingdom and Ireland.

To Write to the Author

If you wish to contact the author or would like more information about this book, please write to the author in care of Llewellyn Worldwide and we will forward your request. Both the author and publisher appreciate hearing from you and learning of your enjoyment of this book and how it has helped you. Llewellyn Worldwide cannot guarantee that every letter written to the author can be answered, but all will be forwarded. Please write to:

J. H. Brennan
℅ Llewellyn Worldwide
2143 Woodale Drive, Dept. 0-7387-0713-9
Woodbury, MN 55125-2989, U.S.A.

Please enclose a self-addressed stamped envelope for reply, or $1.00 to cover costs.
If outside U.S.A., enclose international postal reply coupon.

J. H. BRENNAN

TIBETAN
MAGIC
—+ AND +—
MYSTICISM

Llewellyn Publications
Woodbury, Minnesota

Book design and layout by Steffani Chambers
Cover background art © 2005 by Digital Stock
Cover design by Kevin R. Brown
Llewellyn is a registered trademark of Llewellyn Worldwide, Ltd.
Interior illustrations by Llewellyn Art Department.

ISBN-13: 978-0-7387-0713-6
ISBN-10: 0-7387-0713-9

Llewellyn Publications
A Division of Llewellyn Worldwide, Ltd.
2143 Wooddale Drive, Dept. 0-7387-0713-9
Woodbury, MN 55125-2989, U.S.A.

Printed in the United States of America

ALSO BY J. H. BRENNAN

The Magical I Ching

Magick for Beginners

Time Travel

Magical Use of Thought Forms (with Dolores Ashcroft-Nowicki)

CONTENTS

Part Five: The Tibetan Way of Death

Author's Note

Portions of this book originally appeared in my book *Occult Tibet* (Llewellyn Publications, 2002).

INTRODUCTION: THE MYSTIC CAPITAL OF PLANET EARTH

There are hundreds of thousands of men ready to bear arms. . . . In order to give warning of enemy attacks they use fire and smoke signals. There is a watch-post every hundred li.[1] Their armour and helmets are excellent. When they put them on, their whole body is covered, with holes just for the eyes. Their bow and their sword never leave them. They prize physical strength and despise old age . . .

Military discipline is strict. In battle it is not until the troops in front have been completely wiped out that the troops behind come up into line. They prize death in battle. . . . Those families of whom several generations have died in battle are considered of highest rank. But when someone is defeated in battle or runs away . . . a great crowd will assemble and he is certain to be put to death . . . they feel great shame in this matter and they consider that it is far better to be dead.

As punishments, even for a small fault, they take out the eyes, or cut off the feet or the nose. They give floggings with leather whips just as they see fit and without any regulated number. For prisons, they dig down into the earth several dozens of feet and they keep their prisoners there for two or three years.

When the king dies [five or six of his followers] are killed sacrificially. . . .

---

1. One li in Ancient China is equivalent to 0.3 of a U.S. statute mile.

This description, taken from the official records of Ancient China, clearly refers to a warlike, brutal, barbaric, and bloodthirsty race. But which one? The Mongol hordes destined to terrorize half the world? The dreaded Hun who had already invaded southeastern Europe?

It comes as a shock to discover that the people described are those we now think of as the most gentle on earth—the cheerful, smiling, intensely religious Tibetans.

Contrary to the current image in so many Western minds, Tibet was once a military power that would have put Nazi Germany to shame. Its political history from the seventh to ninth centuries AD was one of almost constant warfare. Nor was Tibet under siege, the innocent victim of a powerful neighbor, as is arguably the case today. Tibet was on the offensive. Her troops pushed farther and farther across the Chinese border, capturing and holding land until on one occasion they even took the Chinese capital. They then went on to isolate China by occupying strategic areas along the routes through Central Asia.

When, during one of the rare periods of peace, Tibet requested copies of the Chinese classics, a high court official petitioned his Emperor in the strongest terms to refuse. There is an undercurrent of panic in his appeal that is obvious to this day:

> How can we give . . . our classics to these barbarian ene-
> mies . . . ? I have heard that these Tibetans have a fierce and
> warlike nature. . . . If they were well-read in the *Book of
> History* they would know about war strategy. If they were
> well-versed in the *Odes* they would know how fighting
> men should be trained to defend their prince. If they were
> well-read in the *Book of Rites*, they would understand sea-
> sonal programmes for the use of arms. If they studied the
> *Tso Chuan* they would know that in warfare it is usual to
> employ deceitful stratagems. . . . In what way would this
> differ from giving weapons to brigands . . . ?

Clearly, Tibet was once an intensely warlike country. But by the time the Chinese invaded in 1950, it possessed just a token army bearing arms more suited to the Middle Ages than the twentieth century. And it had, for centuries, held firmly to a doctrine of nonviolence. What caused the change? How was this murderous culture transformed into a benign, peace-loving nation that managed, for several centuries, to present itself as a spiritual beacon to the world?

Thubten Jigme Norbu thinks he knows the answer. Norbu, former Abbot of Kumbum Monastery and twenty-fourth incarnation of a fifteenth-century Tibetan monk named Tagtser, expressed it in a single sentence: "Chenresig was sent to Tibet to help the Tibetan people."

Chenresig is one of the Enlightened Ones, a group of beings—some with physical bodies, some without—whose sole purpose is the salvation of all living creatures. Among them, Chenresig is an entity so evolved that we—and most Tibetans—would consider him a god. As Tibet's patron deity, he was destined to incarnate during the Year of the Wood Hog (1935) in the body of Norbu's younger brother. Consequently, the child grew up to become the current Dalai Lama.

But Thubten Jigme Norbu was speaking of Chenresig's first appearance several centuries earlier when he said:

> Tibet was chosen not because we were a good people, but because in those days we were given to much fighting and killing and stealing. We were fighting with each other, fighting with our neighbours. Even the Chinese feared us because we were so warlike and powerful. Then, some 2,500 years ago, the Buddha prophesied that Chenresig would come to Tibet and all that changed. We became so peaceful, so unwilling to take even animal life, that our enemies thought they would make us captive and take our country. Several times they nearly succeeded, but Chenresig gave us strength and we had the even greater power of religion.

Western historians tend to assume it was this "greater power of religion" and not some deity that proved the spiritual salvation of Tibet. Buddhism crossed the Himalayas in the seventh century AD and proved such a pervasive influence that the time eventually came when one Tibetan in every four embraced the monastic life.

There is no question at all that the doctrines of the Buddha helped change Tibetan history. All the same, Buddhism alone is no guarantee of a peaceful culture. India, the home of Guatama Buddha, has been to war twice in my lifetime. The killing fields of Cambodia were strewn with Buddhist corpses. Centuries of Buddhism in Japan—although not, admittedly, as the State religion—did little to stop Pearl Harbor.

But perhaps it's unfair to discuss Buddhism as if it were a single creed transplanted, unchanged, from country to country. Far more so than the "religions of the Book" (Judaism, Islam, and Christianity), the doctrines of the Lord Buddha have been modified by the cultures in which they took root. Japanese Zen, for example, bears little resemblance to the Buddhism you might find in Burma.

One modifying influence on the practice of Buddhism in Tibet was the religion in place before it arrived, usually called *Bön* after the name of its presiding priest.

Historically, the origins and early practice of Bön are obscure—surviving records tend to assume more knowledge of its rites than scholars have today—but it is known that the first kings were looked on as divine beings who eventually returned (physically) to the heavens on death, thus avoiding the necessity of a tomb. For the common people, death was death: you simply joined the legion of the dead, who vaguely existed somewhere but no longer played any part in human affairs.

Generally speaking, Bön was far more concerned with this life than the next. It helped its followers discover, usually through divination or astrology, the roots of their illnesses and misfortunes, then went on to advise on how to put things right.

Within the cultural context of Bön, the most likely cause of human tribulations was the mischievous, or sometimes downright malignant, activities of a local sprite, demon, or god.[2] Consequently, the cure tended to be some form of magical ritual. One favorite was the Exchange Rite.

The first step of this popular ceremonial was to identify the troublesome god or demon—something best done by the Bön priest entering trance or studying dreams. Then the priest prepared the items necessary for the ritual. These consisted of a figurine that would represent the patient—or, more accurately, the patient's body—a tree symbol, an arrow, a distaff, several ritual stakes, male and female figures, a plant named *ephedra*, some mustard seed, a model of the patient's house, some examples of the things he wanted badly, and, most important of all, a very curious ceremonial device known as the *nam-mkha*, or "sky."

There were several different forms of nam-mkha. The simplest was a cross made from two bound sticks with colored threads connecting the arms to form a diamond shape, but there were far more elaborate versions, including box or wheel shapes. The purpose of the device was to trap the troublesome entity like a bird in a cage.

Once this was done, the various ritual items were presented as a ransom in an attempt to gain the deity's favor. If the priest had carried out his preparations properly, the symbolic nicknacks would be acknowledged as equivalents of the patient's own property (hence the term *Exchange Rite*) and accepted as a ransom payment. The priest then dismissed the entity by flinging it violently away.

Bön eventually categorized the multitude of spiteful entities that beset struggling humanity. Among them were the *sa-bdag*, or gods of the soil, the *gzhi-dbag*, gods who inhabited conspicuous rock features, and the *klu*, serpent gods who lived in streams and springs. In an agricultural community like Tibet, it was all too easy to fall foul of any of these creatures, who took immediate offense if their land was tilled or buildings raised without the appropriate compensation. It was

---

2. As in Ancient Greece, gods were thought of as capricious, often hostile, and always dangerous.

important to avoid confrontation. In a spiteful mood, all the local divinities could cause sickness and death.

Bön also recognized certain mountains as sacred, inhabited by heroic gods of their own who had, so it was believed, parental ties with early Tibetan kings.

Even the most superficial study of Tibetan Buddhism as practiced in the twentieth century unveils the lurking remnants of the old Bön pantheon, many of its spirits surviving by name, and all a far cry from the cerebral meditations of Guatama Buddha. But then, the Buddhism that entered Tibet in the seventh century AD was itself profoundly changed from the original doctrines.

Buddhism first arose in India near the Nepalese border in the fifth century BC when a closeted young prince named Siddhattha (then just twenty-nine years old) saw a very old man for the first time in his life.

"What's the matter with him?" Siddhattha asked his charioteer.

"Old age," said the charioteer. "Something that comes to us all."

Later, Siddhattha saw someone far gone in illness and asked the same question. The charioteer explained that sickness too was something everybody risked.

Later still, Siddhattha saw a corpse and learned from his charioteer that death was the only real certainty in life.

The experiences convinced the prince that despite occasional highlights, life was essentially suffering, and the only sensible course was to find a way to escape the great Wheel of Reincarnation that kept everyone coming back for more. When he caught sight of a saffron—a robed holy man who seemed completely at peace with the world, Siddhattha recognized a role model. He left the comforts of his palace, his young wife, and their newborn child to become a wandering ascetic searching for the road to *Nirvana*.[3]

---

3. The term is still occasionally equated (quite wrongly) with heaven by Western commentators, and is even more often thought of as a state of bliss. The original meaning is actually "void" or "nothingness," a cessation of suffering that suggests the bliss involved may be analogous to the relief you feel when you stop beating your head against a brick wall.

After nearly starving himself to death, he abandoned the traditional rigors of a holy man's existence (much to the disgust of his followers), started to eat again, and eventually sat himself down beneath a fig tree, vowing not to get up again until he had discovered how to escape the eternal wheel of birth, death, and rebirth.

Using techniques of depth meditation, he achieved enlightenment by the following morning (the term *Buddha* means "Enlightened One") and began to teach the Four Noble Truths: interlinked realizations that all lives, from beggars to kings, are defined by misery; that misery arises solely and directly out of craving; that craving can be eliminated; and that to do so, you need to follow a methodical path. He died at the age of eighty in 483 BC, urging his followers to "work out their own salvation with diligence."

Buddhist doctrine spread first through the cities of the upper Ganges then, encouraged by a third-century BC Emperor, throughout the whole of India. But around the beginning of the Christian Era, it underwent a massive change. A school of thought sprang up that claimed original Buddhist practice was all very well, but actually represented a "lesser way," leading only to a rather selfish sort of salvation for oneself alone.

This, said the new thinkers, was hardly in the spirit of the Buddha himself, who had not been content with just his own salvation, but had gone on to seek salvation for all sentient beings. While he may have taught the lesser way to those weak-spirited disciples incapable of doing any better, it was clear that the only sensible path for a perfect follower was to try to become a Buddha himself, fully enlightened, and, like his role model Guatama, determined to work for the enlightenment and salvation of all. Those who subscribed to this ambitious doctrine liked to refer to themselves as followers of the *Mahayana,* or Great Way.

It was the Great Way, itself modified by more than two centuries of Tantric practice,[4] that was imported into Tibet around the time

---

4. A set of psycho-spiritual and physical disciplines that promised power and enlightenment, but also diverged from the original Buddhist message.

Buddhism was under siege in its native India.[5] The idea of working toward Buddhahood clearly had a strong appeal for the Tibetan temperament.

When he analyzed the original emergence of Bön in his country, Abbot Norbu commented:

> Every traveller who has set foot in Tibet has commented on the wild countryside. . . . It is a country that can be so still and quiet and so beautiful that even we who have been born in it . . . are affected strongly. [But] just as it can be quiet, it can also be so tumultuous that it seems as though the world were coming to an end. . . . If the country is powerful in its quiet moments, it is something much more than powerful when it is black. . . . Living in a world like this, it is difficult not be become dominated by it.[6]

There seems little doubt that Bön emerged in reaction to the country of its birth exactly as the Abbot suggests—it is far easier to accept spirits of the earth and serpent divinities in a wilderness like Tibet than it would be in a New York apartment. But the newly-planted Buddhism was to share the same fate. Indeed, there are so many similarities between the two religions that it is often difficult to tell them apart. Thubten Jigme Norbu again:

> There is no way of telling whether a man is a Bönpoba or a Buddhist when you meet him. His clothes, his manner of speech, his behaviour, all are the same as our own.[7]

Like Buddhism, the Bön religion had its monasteries. Both types were organized in the same way. Monks in each took exactly the

---

5. So much so that it eventually all but disappeared from the land that gave it birth.

6. Quoted from *Tibet: Its History, Religion and People*, by Thubten Jigme Norbu and Colin Turnbull (London: Pelican Books, 1972).

7. Ibid.

same number of vows: 253. It is clear that the modern version of Bön (which was already beginning to modify itself when Buddhism arrived) borrowed from Buddhism. It is equally clear that Buddhism borrowed from Bön. Until the Chinese invasion, the (Buddhist) government was a reincarnatory monarchy whose decisions were guided by spirit voices speaking through a State Oracle. Certain mountains were still considered sacred. The local gods of wild places were still honored. You could still see the nam-mkha sky cross in ceremonial use.

But side by side with the influence of Bön, another influence came into play—the great Himalayan mountain chain. In a very real sense, the Himalayas created Tibet. They form a barrier that stands twenty-four thousand feet high and stretches fifteen hundred miles from east to west. It is a barrier that blocks the monsoon winds and has turned much of Tibet—and indeed Central Asia as a whole—into a chill desert. It also put a stop to humanity's ancient migrations across the Central Asian steppes and led to an isolation that has been the country's most dominant cultural characteristic for centuries. Until the Chinese invasion, you could generally count the number of foreign residents in Tibet on the fingers of one hand.

A land will always sculpt its people. If isolation has been the country's predominant cultural characteristic, its most obvious physical characteristic is thin air—something that has profound implications for those who live there. When London *Times* correspondent Perceval Landon visited Phag Ri, Tibet's highest settlement, in 1904, he found a ramshackle village of listless inhabitants.

The characteristic listlessness sprang from oxygen deprivation. At eighteen thousand feet, Phag Ri was not only the highest town in the country, but in the world. Even Tibetans found it difficult to cope. Phag Ri is, of course, an extreme example, but oxygen levels across the whole of Tibet are so low that acclimatized Tibetans refer to their experience when visiting the plains of India as "breathing soup."

There is a well-known phenomenon in the world of high-altitude mountaineering. Those who engage in the sport call it the "unseen companion." Climber after climber, including several engaged in Everest expeditions, has reported the eerie sensation of being accompanied by something or someone on the final stages of their climb, even though no one was actually there. Rather more controversially, one or two have even claimed that the unseen presence helped them when they got into trouble, protected them against the worst effects of blizzards, and guided their footsteps back to safety.

The occultist Aleister Crowley, no mean mountaineer himself, learned that the unseen companion had a negative side when he tackled Himalayan peak K2, known locally as Kanchenjunga and the second highest mountain in the world. Although Crowley was courageous to the point of stupidity when climbing, he met with something on Kanchenjunga that terrified him. At least one of his biographers[8] has assumed Crowley was personifying the mountain—a particularly treacherous peak that has killed a number of climbers—when he referred to the "Kanchenjunga Demon," but it is far more likely that he was speaking about an experience of the unseen companion.

The phenomenon manifests when mountaineers venture into high altitudes without oxygen equipment, or when their equipment fails. This has led to the assumption that the experience is essentially a hallucination brought on by oxygen deprivation—a variation on the altitude sickness experienced by some tourists visiting destinations like Nepal. The locals take a different view. To them, the unseen companion is exactly what it seems to be—a disembodied entity that attaches itself, for good or ill, to those who enter its domain.

It is tempting to dismiss the local view as superstition, but perhaps a little rash. Aldous Huxley, the British intellectual, experimented with mescaline and subsequently wrote a fascinating account of the experience in which he discussed the theory of "mind-at-large." According to this theory, the human mind is not generated by the physical brain, as so many Western scientists assume. Rather, it is something above and beyond the body that is aware of reality at a far deeper level than

---

8. The British author John Symonds.

most of us experience. The brain acts as a "reducing valve," filtering out those impressions that are not useful for the job of survival. Mystical consciousness is all very well, but so seductive that if you had it all the time, you might easily walk under a bus.

Huxley theorized that psychedelic substances like mescaline, and many spiritual pursuits, including yoga breathing, all reduce the efficiency of the brain as a filter, allowing more impressions of mind-at-large to flood in. Far from being hallucinatory, these impressions are intimations of reality levels we cannot normally access.

During the latter part of the 1960s, a series of experiments carried out by the distinguished British neurophysiologist Dr. W. Grey Walter lent indirect support to the theory of mind-at-large. Although his findings have been largely ignored, his work showed conclusively that mind, whatever it may be, cannot be a product of the brain.

Grey Walter's experimental procedure was based on the fact that the human brain generates measurable electrical signals. He attached electrodes to the scalps of volunteers over the area of the frontal cortex. These amplified electrical activity and sent the signals on to a specially constructed machine. The subject had a button before him that he could press to cause an interesting scene to appear on a TV screen.

When you decide to take any physical action—including the pressing of a button—there is a twenty micro-volt electrical surge across your frontal cortex. Specialists call this a "readiness wave." Grey Walter amplified this readiness wave so that it could trigger the TV picture a fraction of a second before the button was actually pressed.

Subjects usually figured out what was happening fairly quickly and trained themselves to "will" the pictures onto the screen without touching the button. For this trick to work, the subject had to duplicate his or her mindset in pressing the button. Once the knack was developed, subjects could will pictures onto the screen directly, then dismiss them with the relevant thought when finished.

The appearance of screen pictures was not mind acting directly on matter since the switch was triggered by the amplified electrical surge originating in the subject's brain. But once subjects learned how to produce the pictures without pressing the button, their minds *were* directly influencing matter—the physical matter of their own brains. A decision of the mind, applied in a particular way, was all it took to change the electrical potential of the frontal cortex.

Grey Walter's experiments showed conclusively that it is the mind that controls the brain and not the other way around.[9] The implications are far-reaching. Among them is the realization that mind-at-large can no longer be dismissed as a philosophical fantasy.

In the Tibetan context, this may mean that the country's basic geographical features—notably its thin air—created generations of people who were constitutionally attuned to levels of reality normally hidden from the rest of us. This contributed to the development of Bön, the modification of Buddhism, the rise of a profound mysticism, and the appearance of an occult practice that partook of both religions.

The evolutionary result is apparent in the Tibetan language, which is choc-a-bloc with different terms for (to the average Westerner) incomprehensibly subtle levels of meditation and trance. Generations of monks, sequestered in monasteries that sometimes reached the size of small towns, devoted their lives to an investigation of the human mind that is literally unparalleled anywhere on earth. Where Western psychology chose the path of theory and investigation, these men became psychonauts, mounting a personal exploration of inner space that carried them to realms of strangeness ranging from the development of near miraculous powers to the contemplation of ultimate reality.

This book explores their findings. This book examines the astounding magic and mysticism of Tibet.

---

9. The conclusion was confirmed in 2000 when scientific research in Scotland showed that in rare cases where flatline (brain dead) patients were revived, many reported memories, indicating that their minds had somehow survived the (temporary) demise of their brains.

Part One:

TIβETAN

DISCOVERIES

CHAPTER ONE

THE KHOR–LO SYSTEM

The New Age movement went a long way toward introducing the concept of *chakras* to a widespread Western audience. They were postulated to be a series of subtle vortices by means of which a universal life force was received, transformed, and distributed throughout the human body.

But mainstream Western biology staunchly refused to recognize their reality. They couldn't be seen, they couldn't be dissected, and, therefore, they didn't exist. Then the Japanese scientist Hiroshi Motoyama decided to test the idea experimentally. Placing his subjects in a lead-lined booth to screen out extraneous radiation, he set out to measure energy levels generated in specific areas of the human body. He found that there was indeed a high-frequency energy discharge at the traditional chakra locations, but, more significantly, when subjects with meditation experience were asked to "open" a particular chakra,[10] the energy level increased when compared to that of a control. When one woman was required to open her heart chakra, a photoelectric cell registered increased light levels as well.

Mainstream Western biology ignored his findings and continues to deny the existence of the chakras.

---

10. Usually a matter of visualization.

The situation is very different in the East. The earliest mention of chakras occurs in the literature of Hindu yoga, but it's possible—even likely—that the system was discovered independently in China, which has experience of subtle body energies through a practice of acupuncture stretching back millennia.

In India, the chakra system was adopted and modified in mainstream Buddhism and may well have been carried with Buddhism into Tibet. The Tibetans have labeled the centers *khor-lo,* a term that translates as "wheel." The word *chakra* comes from Sanskrit and also means "wheel." But despite the coincidence, there are indications that the khor-lo may have been discovered independently in Tibet as well.

While there are hundreds of minor chakras, the basic Hindu system lists seven major centers. These are located along the midline of the body, centered on the spinal column. In Tibet, however, only five khor-lo are recognized. As we'll see, some, but not all, equate directly with the Hindu chakras, while others combine two chakras into a single khor-lo. This suggests the possibility of independent discovery with chakra areas that have an energy overlap sensed directly and classified as one. But whether original discoveries or experiential modifications, the khor-lo of Tibet have had wide-reaching implications in areas as diverse as medicine and dreaming.

To understand the Tibetan system, it is useful to have some grasp of the original Hindu teachings about the seven major chakras. Under clairvoyant observation, each one has the appearance of a multicolored spoked wheel, or, more poetically, a lotus flower. There is the distinct impression that the centers are in movement, perhaps spinning. These impressions have been systematized so that Hindu doctrine asserts each chakra has its own predominant color, number of "petals," and speed of spin, or energy vibration. All these factors are influenced by the health of the individual. In sickness, the chakras grow cloudy and their spin slows or becomes irregular.

Over the years, yogis working with the chakras have built up a series of associations with each one. These include specific sounds, geometric shapes, elements, and even letters of the alphabet. The table that follows will allow you easy access to this chakra information from the original Indian viewpoint.

Hindu Chakra System

Chakra	root	sacral	solar plexus	heart	throat	brow	crown
Location	base of spine	four finger-widths below the navel	at or just above the navel	midway between shoulder blades in center of chest	throat	between the eye-brows	just above the top of the head
Physical	sacral plexus	hypogastric plexus	solar plexus	cardiac plexus	cervic plexus	medulla oblongata	brain/ pituitary
Controls	external generative organs	internal organs of reproduction and secretion	digestive system	blood circulation	respiratory system	automatic nervous system	volitional nervous system
Hindu Name	muladhara	svadhisthana	manipurna	anahata	visuddha	ajna	sahasrara
Petals	4	6	10	12	16	96	972
Color	yellow	white	red	gray-blue	white	—	—
Element	earth	water	fire	air	ether	—	—
Sound	lam	vam	ram	yam	ham	ah (short)	om
Shape	square	crescent	triangle	hexagram	circle	—	—

Although useful, the table is necessarily limited. For example, to state that the root *muladhara* chakra controls the external generative organs does little justice to the far-reaching influence of this center. Through its links with the sacral plexus of the cerebro-spinal system, it controls the lower limbs as well. As we proceed upward through the centers, we can see that the influence of each becomes increasingly pervasive.

The sacral *svadhisthana* influences the bladder, lower intestin, urinary ducts, and the process of elimination.

The solar plexus *manipurna* influences the stomach, upper intestine, gallbladder, bladder, gall ducts, seminal ducts in a man, liver, kidneys, and spleen. Like the sacral, it exerts influence on the urinary ducts.

The heart *anahata* influences the physical heart and to some extent the lungs, hence blood constituents as well as blood flow.

The throat *visuddha* is the main influence on the lungs and respiratory system in general, and also controls the upper limbs.

The brow *ajna* controls the sense organs, having a special relationship with eyes, ears, nose, tongue, and skin.

The crown *sahasrara* has perhaps the most pervasive influence of all. The universal life force is believed to enter the body through this chakra and is then channeled downward to the other chakras, which transform it into the specific type of energy required for their individual functions. The chakra itself is believed to be of a different order than the others, existing, so to speak, on a higher dimension of reality and forming a link with cosmic consciousness. At a more physical level, its associations with the brain and the mind allow it direct or indirect control of every bodily function.

Even the sounds given in the table are no more than the "central" associated syllable. The chakras are visualized as lotus flowers, each with a specific number of petals. Each petal has its own associated sound. The six-petaled lotus of svadhisthana, for example, has the central sound of *vam,* but each petal (energy stream) generates its own harmonic: *bam, bham, mam, yam, ram,* and *lam.* Although credited with 972 energy streams, the crown is often thought of as expressing the infinite variety produced by the interaction of all the harmonics of all the petals of all the remaining chakras.[11] The specific characteristics of each center has led to symbolic associations with

---

11. In actuality, the number of harmonics generated by the crown chakra is not infinite, but it is very large indeed. Assuming the figures given for the energy streams of the other chakras are accurate, I would calculate a total of 4,423,680 crown harmonics.

Hindu deities and animals. The heart chakra, for example, has a prime characteristic of motion, hence the choice of a deer as its symbol, since a deer's most obvious characteristic is its speed.

Alongside the chakra associations with physical processes and symbols that relate to the nature and function of the chakra itself, the linkages extend into broad behavior patterns and mental states. The muladhara is the foundation of the instinct for self-preservation and what might be called, without negative connotations, your animal nature. The svadhisthana has an influence on general health and well-being. The manipurna is linked to the emotions and often seems to be a factor in trance mediumship. The anahata is associated with higher consciousness and unconditional love. The visuddha is involved with effective communication, creativity, and, curiously enough, some states of expanded consciousness. The ajna relates to intelligence, intuition, psychic powers, and enlightenment. The sahasrara is believed to show the individual's level of spiritual evolution. It is involved in cosmic consciousness and the ultimate states of enlightenment.

From all this you will readily appreciate that the Hindu doctrine of the chakra system is complex indeed. The Tibetan khor-lo system is scarcely less so.

Apart from terminology, the most obvious difference between the two is that the Tibetans recognize only five major khor-lo, rather than the Hindu seven. In Tibet, the root "khor-lo" is known as *sangna,* the "Secret Place," and combines the svadhisthana and muladhara chakras of Hindu yoga. The Secret Place is concerned with the whole process of reproduction, while the digestive/elimination functions of the svadhisthana tend to be linked with the solar plexus khor-lo above.

At the opposite end of the scale, the crown and brow chakras are also combined to form a single khor-lo center called *hdab-ston,* the "Thousand-Petaled Lotus." The merger is interesting since the ajna chakra of the brow relates to the legendary "third eye" widely believed in the Orient to be the seat of visionary experience. Tibetans, as we shall see, do not subscribe to the prevalent Western idea that visions are necessarily subjective. They believe that at least some visionary states represent a direct experience of other levels of reality. The following table gives basic khor-lo references.

But the khor-lo can never usefully be studied in isolation. In Tibetan thought, they are seen as aspects—albeit fairly critical aspects—of an energy system that pervades the entire human body.

Tibetan Chakra System

Chakra	genital	navel	heart	throat	head
Location	centered at base of spine between genitals and anus	at navel	center of chest at level of the physical heart	throat	crown of head extending over forehead
Endocrine System	gonads or ovaries	possibly pancreas	adrenals	thyroid	pineal and pituitary
Tibetan Name	Wheel of the Preservation of Happiness	Wheel of Transmutation	Wheel of Phenomena	Wheel of Enjoyment	Wheel of Bliss
Energy Spokes	32	64	8	16	32
Color	green	yellow	blue	red	white
Element	air	earth	water	fire	ether or space
Sound	ha	swa	hum	ah	om
Direction	north	south	east	west	center
Buddha Quality	infallible	origin of jewels	imperturbable	boundless light	making forms visible
Buddha Aspect	activity	quality	mind	speech	whole body
Mentation	concepts	feelings	consciousness	perceptions	forms
Stupidity (Poison)	jealousy	pride	anger	desire	ignorance
Wisdom (Transmuted Poison)	all-accomplishing wisdom	equalizing wisdom	mirror wisdom	discriminating wisdom	absolute wisdom
Animal	bird	horse	elephant	peacock	lion

CHAPTER TWO

THE RLUNG SYSTEM

According to the tenets of Tibetan medicine, an embryo evolves a complex energy system during its initial eight weeks in the womb.

First to develop are the three main channels (*rtsa*) of life energy. The central channel (*dbu-ma*) originates on the top of the head just beneath the soft spot on the skull and runs down through the spine to a space located four finger-widths below the navel. The right channel (*ro-ma*) branches off from the center just above the eyebrows, then runs parallel to it about an inch or so away until it rejoins the center just below the navel. The left channel (*rkyang-ma*) exactly mirrors the right on the other side of the midline.

While the center channel corresponds in its location to the spinal cord, it is, like the other two, a nonphysical vein of energy invisible to normal sight. Tibetans believe, however, that the channels are discernable to clairvoyant vision and consequently have recorded detailed descriptions of them. The center channel is hollow, luminous, blue in color, and approximately the size of an arrow shaft. The side channels are a little thinner, but also hollow and luminous. They are different colors, red and white, but which is which varies depending on whether you are male or female. For a boy the right channel is white, the left red. The reverse is the case for a girl.

Once these three major channels are established in the embryo, minor rtsa begin to form, creating a network that eventually stretches throughout the entire body. Some Tibetan sources number seventy-two thousand of these minor channels, but this may be more symbolic than actual, simply suggesting there are a great many.

Although the three major channels are often visualized as running in straight parallel lines, this is simply a convenience. In actuality, the two side channels intertwine with the central channel. Their crossing points mark the khor-lo energy centers. The drawing below indicates the relationship and interactions between them.

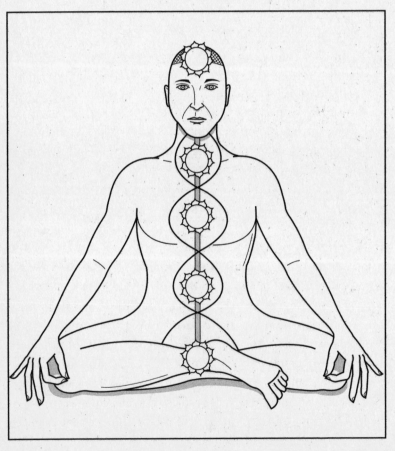

Khor-lo centers and rtsa channels.

Some esoteric systems consider the psychic channels and the energies that flow through them to be much the same thing, but Tibetan doctrine differentiates between the two. The channels are clearly described as rtsa, energy courses analogous to a water pipe, electrical wire, or bed of a river. The energies themselves are known as *rlung*, which translates as "airs" or "forces."

A third element in the equation is the *thig-li*,[12] an umbrella term for certain subtle essences believed to pervade the individual. There are two types of thig-li: relative and absolute. Relative thig-lis are generated from a single fundamental thig-li in the heart chakra that contains both the essence of the life force and the essence of the five elements. The relative thig-lis are like drops of this central essence that find their way into various parts of the body via the rtsa channels. Tibetan doctrine speaks of a red "mother" drop that moves downward along the central channel and a white "father" drop that moves upward. Relative thig-lis never leave the channels, but having established themselves in their specific locations function as the supports of life and awareness.

The absolute thig-li is quite different. It is neither a drop nor a series of drops and it has no particular location. Instead, it pervades every channel, chakra, energy stream, and relative essence throughout the entire system. Lamas think of it as the self-illuminating, changeless, enlightened mind of primordial wisdom, which, unfortunately, goes completely unrecognized in most of us.

Taken together, these three—the rtsa with their khor-lo, the rlung and the thig-li—are the major components of a subtle body that interpenetrates the physical and is believed to form the crucial link between it and what Tibetans think of as the *dorje*,[13] the unchanging "diamond body" that represents an individual's essential Buddha nature or divine spark.

---

12. Sometimes transliterated as *thig-le* or even *thigle*.

13. A confusing use of the word, since a *dorje* is also a ritual implement. The term means "thunderbolt" or "diamond," hence its special usage to describe a subtle body.

These various elements interact with the physical body and the familiar processes of the mind to form the totality of the human being. From the Tibetan perspective, the physical body depends on the rtsa psychic channels. The rtsa in turn depend on the rlung, or energies. The rlung depend on the mind. For a real grasp of Tibetan perspective, it is useful to run this sequence backward. When you do, you realize that the mind (usually by means of generated emotions) controls the body's energies, which control the channels, which control the multitude of processes within the physical body. Thus the mind controls everything—but not necessarily at a conscious level. The Tibetans say the rlung energies are like an untamed horse. The mind is the rider, but the conscious mind has to learn how to get the horse under control.

The mind itself is not entirely what we experience it to be. Tibetan philosophy agrees with Western psychology that there are whole areas of mentation of which we are normally unaware. But the Tibetans go further by postulating subtle levels of mind and mind/energy interactions unsuspected in the West. This brings us back to the concept of absolute thig-li. Although most of us experience our mind as somehow located inside the skull behind the eyes, Tibetans believe the absolute essence of mind pervades the entire body. It is the link with our Buddha-nature.

The relationship between mind and the body's subtle energy systems is one of the most interesting aspects of Tibetan doctrine. Speaking at the fourth biennial Mind and Life Conference in Dharamsala, India, in 1992, the Dalai Lama touched on the relationship when he maintained that neither mind nor consciousness were things in themselves, since there were actually many subtle levels and degrees of mind and consciousness. What he referred to as "gross consciousness"—the consciousness we experience in our everyday waking state—depended on the brain for its existence. So long as the brain continued to function, gross consciousness was maintained. Once an individual flatlined and brain death occurred, the familiar experience of consciousness could no longer arise.

So far, this is in accord with Western neuroscience, but the Dalai Lama then made reference to the idea that a subtle "essence of mind" existed independently of the brain and pervaded the body's energy system, notably at the heart khor-lo. This meant that from the Tibetan perspective, mind could survive brain death, at least for as long as the energy system remained functioning. In fact, as we shall see in the final chapters of this book, Tibetans accept that a very subtle essence of mind continues to survive even when the entire physical basis of the energy system has ceased to exist—when, that is, the flesh has rotted and the bones have crumbled into dust.

As you will probably have realized by now, Tibetan doctrines of the subtle energies are by no means easy to follow. Furthermore, the variations of the Tibetan khor-lo system can be confusing to anyone familiar with Hindu teachings on the subject. But an understanding of energy theory is vital to an understanding of Tibetan magical and mystical practice. For it is the manipulation of the energy system that underlies almost every marvel Tibet has ever produced.

CHAPTER THREE

GURUS AND CHELAS

Transmission of Tibet's great spiritual tradition has, for several centuries, relied partly on the study and ceremonial of the country's many monasteries,[14] and partly on a *guru-chela* relationship, which often formed part of monastic practice, but could just as easily exist outside of it.

The term *guru*, defined as a spiritual teacher, is well enough known in the West. The term *chela* is somewhat less so. In esoteric Buddhism, it is defined as "a novice qualifying for initiation," but it is often used simply to denote the disciple of a particular guru.

In Tibet, there is a strong belief that anyone embarking on the spiritual path does not alone benefit from direct contact with his or her guru, but also from the guru's teacher and the teacher's teachers in turn, reaching back through time to the original mentor—in Buddhism, the Buddha himself in his celestial form.

This concept is not just a recognition that the doctrine has been passed on through many generations: the chela will typically think of the daisy-chain as a band of teachers, all still very much alive, although most no longer incarnate, who are aiding the student in his

---

14. At least prior to the Chinese invasion.

or her endeavors. To this congregation might be added one or more deities with whom the student has a special affinity.

As we shall see a little later, one important spiritual exercise requires the chela to visualize the whole succession of discarnate gurus, in ascending order of importance, one beyond the other in a vertical line above the student's head or along the central energy channel of his or her body. The chain of spiritual command is clearly defined, with the supreme guru (Vajra-Dhara) uppermost. The chela is then required to acknowledge the entire chain in prayer.

The prayer formula is not standard, but rather something passed directly to the pupil by his or her immediate incarnate guru. One example, preserved in the ancient texts, goes as follows:

> *Unto Thee, of the pure and holy Truth Realm from where there is no more fall into incarnation,*
> *O Lord, wielder of the dorje, essence of the sixth Dhyani Buddha,*
> *I, thy child, pray in humility and faith.*
> *Grant me perfected practice on the Path of Pho-wa*
> *And, in the glorious Divine Realm,*
> *May I attain the unchanging state of the primordial Dharma-Kaya.*

> *Unto thee of the Paradise Realm,*
> *O Lords Tilopa, Naropa, and Marpa, Father and Sons,*
> *I, thy child, pray in humility and faith.*
> *Grant me perfected practice on the Path of Pho-wa*
> *And, in the glorious Divine Realm,*
> *May I attain the unchanging state of the primordial Dharma-Kaya.*

> *Unto thee, of the rays of realization that our world has no reality,*

O thou, the venerable Milarepa, whose graciousness can never be repaid,
   I, thy child, pray in humility and faith.
   Grant me perfected practice on the Path of Pho-wa
   And, in the glorious Divine Realm,
   May I attain the unchanging state of the primordial Dharma-Kaya.

Unto thee, of the rays of primal truth, the Foundation of all Foundations—Mind,
   O thou, Shakya-Shrl, the unhampered manifestation of the power of mind,
   I, thy child, pray in humility and faith.
   Grant me perfected practice on the Path of Pho-wa
   And, in the glorious Divine Realm,
   May I attain the unchanging state of the primordial Dharma-Kaya.

Unto Thee, seated on a lotus-throne above my crown chakra and beneath the lunar disk.
   0 Thou Root Guru, whose graciousness can never be repaid,
   I, thy child, pray in humility and faith.
   Grant me perfected practice on the Path of Pho-wa
   And, in the glorious Divine Realm,
   May I attain the unchanging state of the primordial Dharma-Kaya.

Being moved by my faith and humility,
   May the Line of Gurus, above my head, be at last dissolved in light,
   Becoming now the Lord Himself, Dorje-Chang, Guru Divine.

Several terms used in this prayer require a little explanation.

The dorje in line three translates as "thunderbolt," but refers, in this instance, to an important ceremonial implement, a mystic scepter. The *Dorje-Chang*, the deity who wields the scepter, is the first of the Celestial Buddhas in Tibetan tradition and overlord of the five Dhyani (Wisdom) Buddhas.

Pho-wa is a term for which there is no direct English-language equivalent. It refers primarily to the transfer of consciousness from the after-death state to the prenatal womb state in preparation for an individual's next incarnation. But if consciousness is routinely—and naturally—transferred this way during the eternal wheel of birth, death, and rebirth, Tibetans also believe it can, with effort, be transferred to other, higher states, notably the Clear Light of Nirvana.

Furthermore, once a guru has achieved a certain state for himself or herself, the term *pho-wa* is used to denote the direct transference of the guru's own consciousness level to his or her pupil. This is sometimes seen as a telepathic passing-on of knowledge, but it actually goes beyond that. Although some knowledge transfer may be involved, consciousness and knowledge are not the same thing. Tibetan spiritual doctrines link an individual's consciousness with his or her energy system, which means spiritual evolution is reflected in the physical body and not just in the intellect. By a process analogous to sympathetic vibration—set a pendulum swinging and it will tend to set off any other pendulum in its vicinity—the chela's state can be attuned to that of his or her guru, a transfer of consciousness *level* rather than consciousness *content*. The phrase "perfected practice on the Path of Pho-wa" refers to this process.

The term *Dharma-Kaya*, which appears in the final line of most verses, literally translates as "divine body of truth." In Buddhism, the *dharma* is a convenient umbrella term for the teachings of the Lord Buddha, but the use of the adjective "primordial" in the prayer changes the sense very subtly. The aspiration expressed is not simply to know truth, but to *be* truth. Consequently, one enters a state in which one recognizes the reality behind appearances and one's own unity with it.

Finally, the term translated as "root guru" refers to the (usually human) teacher seen as the fundamental link to the chain of supra-human entities guiding the student. A Tibetan will typically identify his or her root guru with no more trouble than you might identify your boss at work. It is the person, man or woman, who first set the student on the spiritual path, his or her sacred role model.

Although not necessarily the most highly evolved of the guru chain, the root guru always holds a unique place in the heart of the chela and is the subject of a special prayer:

> *Honor to all who prevailed in Unity!*
> *0 Thou, Embodiment of all Protectors,*
> *Lord of the Mystic Faith entire,*
> *Lord of all that makes my Refuge, now and hereafter,*
> *Thou, whose graciousness can never be repaid,*
> *Thou knowest, 0 Root Guru of surpassing kindness,*
> *Thou knowest, I pray to Thee from the depths of my heart*
> *That I may speedily attain Perfection on the Path of Pho-wa*
> *O Thou, in the Akanishtha Heaven, the emanation of the*
> *Pure Realm of the Dharma-Kaya,*
> *Grant me thy inspiration that self-knowledge, the*
> *unchanging state of the Dharma-Kaya, may be attained.*

It is noteworthy that "the unchanging state of the Dharma-Kaya"—awareness of and participation in the Ultimate Reality—is equated in the prayer with self-knowledge. For the Tibetan mystic, psychological processes and spiritual states form a seamless continuum. In the penultimate line of the prayer, the term translated as "inspiration" goes beyond any idea that the guru is simply setting an example. A more active process is referred to, with the guru believed to broadcast psychic influences to his pupil.

As an aid to pho-wa, the transference of a consciousness level from guru to chela, specific meditation and visualization practices are recommended to follow the prayer forms already given.

The work begins with a conscious affirmation of the fundamental principle embodied in Mahayana practice—the desire to lead all sentient beings to perfection. It is this end alone that justifies pho-wa.

The meditation associated with this affirmation includes some vivid visualization practice and runs along the lines:

> *My guru is the embodiment of the Threefold Refuge.*[15] *He stands before me now in the firmament. Innumerable sentient beings, myself included, are taking refuge in him, until every one of us will achieve the essence of perfection and lead every living creature to the attainment of the highest path.*

This portion of the meditation concludes with a visualization of the guru being absorbed into the body and spirit of the chela. The chela is then instructed to think of himself as becoming empty in body and mind, a complete stilling of the mental processes so that all thought ceases.

The cessation of mental chatter is, of course, the aim of many forms of meditation and yoga practice—one of which we shall examine in some detail later. In the present context, it is believed that once the target state is achieved, the familiar thought-flow ceases to obstruct deeper, spiritual effects. Out of the void there will emerge spontaneously a vision of the Vajra-Dakini, a goddess who embodies spiritual energy and intellect.

This deity is frequently depicted in Tibetan art as bright ruby red in color with a visible third eye in the middle of her forehead. In her right hand she holds a gleaming curved knife high above her head to cut off completely all intrusive thought processes. In her left hand she holds a blood-filled human skull against her breast. On the head of the goddess is a tiara made from five dried human skulls, while around her neck is a necklace of fifty human heads dripping blood.

---

15. A standard reference in Buddhism worldwide, where followers claim to take refuge in the Buddha, his teachings, and the Buddhist priesthood.

She wears arm-bands, wrist-bands, and anklets, but her only other item of adornment is a Mirror of Karma breastplate held in place by double strings of beads made from human bones that circle her waist and pass over her shoulders. There is a long staff in the crook of her left arm and a flamelike aura around her whole form. The goddess is dancing with her right leg bent and the foot lifted up while her left foot tramples a prostrate human.

When this fearsome goddess appears, the chela is instructed vividly to visualize the median energy channel of her body—straight and hollow, white on the outside, red on the inside, and the approximate thickness of an arrow. The lower end, which is closed during the individual's lifetime, terminates four finger-widths below her navel, while the upper end opens up from the crown chakra at the top of the head.

A portion of the channel naturally extends through the heart, where the chela is instructed to visualize a four-petaled lotus.[16] On the pericarp of the flower (where the fruit is formed) a pale pink dot should be visualized, symbolizing the embodiment of breath and mind inseparably united.

By this point, it is clear that while the goddess emerges spontaneously once normal thought-processes are stilled, she is not exactly what we would think of in the West as an objective entity. Her form and (as we shall see in a moment) her actions are under the control of the meditator. This is our first introduction to the interesting Tibetan idea that deities, demons, and several other classifications of spiritual entities are essentially mental phenomena. But it would be a mistake for the Western reader to assume this means the entities are purely subjective.

It would appear that our commonplace—and clear-cut—distinction between subjective and objective is much more blurred in Tibetan philosophy. There's little doubt that Tibetans believe they can call up a deity by an act of imagination, but at the same time the deity itself is clearly not considered "imaginary" in the familiar sense of the

---

16. Interestingly, this differs from the twelve-petaled lotus of the heart chakra in Hindu tradition.

word. It's as if the mental picture acts as a temporary body that is activated by the spirit of a deity whose real home is somewhere "beyond."

These are difficult ideas for the Western mind to follow, and we shall return to them later in this book. But for the moment it should be noted that Tibetan perceptions of our inner processes are by no means identical to those of Western psychology.

As the exercise in pho-wa continues, the chela is instructed to imagine a variation of the guru chain mentioned in the earlier prayers. Above the crown of the chela's head he should see his root guru as before, but now having taken the form of the Dorje-Chang himself. This supreme Buddha is traditionally visualized as seated cross-legged on a lion throne. Beyond the pseudo Dorje-Chang comes the line of gurus in the pho-wa tradition, each seated, cross-legged, one above the other, extending back to the original Dorje-Chang.[17]

The visualization has a strong emotional element. The chela is instructed to manifest his faith "until the very hairs of thy body stand on end and tears course down thy cheeks." Once in this mood, the chela should pray to his gurus in the form given at the beginning of this chapter.

When the prayer is completed, the exercise becomes a little complicated. The chela is instructed to imagine that those in the chain of gurus who were once, or still are, in human form begin to gradually dissolve into a glorious radiance that finally merges into the body of the root guru (who, you will recall, is being visualized in the form of Dorje-Chang). The pupil should then pray fervently to the root guru as many times as he can.

The repeated prayer is followed by another series of complex visualizations that are typically Tibetan in that they embody a belief in the power of sound and in the representation of certain sounds within

---

17. Thus the line begins and ends with a mental representation of the Supreme Celestial Buddha.

written Tibetan. The visualizations begin when the chela imagines the syllable *hum* in the heart of his guru.

In Hindu belief, a vibrationary *hum* is thought to be the fundamental sound of the universe itself. In Tibet—at least in this particular meditation—it embodies the essence of mind of the Buddha and, by extension, of all Buddhas. (The two may not be entirely different, as we shall see. There is a strong belief throughout Tibet that the mind of the Buddha encompasses the Ultimate Reality on which all manifestation rests.)

The written representation of *hum* in Tibetan looks like this:

In the heart of the guru it is visualized in blue, representing an unchanging eternity, and seen as emitting the radiance of the five Wisdom Buddhas. As the chela visualizes, he is required to utter, loudly and sharply, a sound written in the ancient texts as *heeg!* The chela should simultaneously imagine that the dot in the heart of the Vajra-Dakini is rising up like a bubble into the guru's heart, where it blends with the *hum* syllable to create a state of mystical unity. Once the chela senses this state, he is instructed to enter and remain in it for a period of time before moving on to the rest of the exercise, a brief end sequence in which he utters the sound *ka* and imagines the dot falling back to its own place in the heart of the Vajra-Dakini.

One text promises that successful use of the exercise is accompanied by quite specific physical signs—a swelling at the crown of the head that tends to ooze blood and a thin, yellowish secretion. The scalp at this point thins to such a degree that it can actually be pierced by a stalk of grass. An advanced practitioner should be able to produce these signs after just twenty-one repetitions, while even an unskilled meditator should see results within a single day.

When the signs appear, the chela is advised to stop the earlier practice and replace it with a visualization of his root guru transformed into the Buddha of Infinite Light. This figure holds in his hands an urn (known as the Urn of Life) and pours out a mystic liquid to fill the chela's body and upper chakras, thus granting the boon of limitless life.

To aid the process, the chela is required to chant the mantra *aum ah ma ra ni ji van ti ye svah hah,* then visualize the Buddha as transformed into a radiant orb that the chela absorbs into himself. The instructions conclude:

> *Then, rising up, as a god riseth up, or as doth a bird in flight that leaveth no track, thou shouldst continue in the State of the Reality of the Incomprehensible Dharma-Kaya and pray that thou shalt realize this Highest State.*

From all this it will be clear that reverence of the guru—or even the chain of gurus—is not an end in itself, but a means to an end. The goal has always been the realization of the reality behind appearances, often described in terms of pure consciousness and experienced as limitless light.[18]

This is a goal we shall return to again and again in our exploration of Tibetan mysticism and magic.

---

18. Interestingly, the concept of limitless light as a symbol of the reality behind appearances is shared by Jewish Qabalists.

CHAPTER FOUR

STRANGE POWERS

In 1956, the Chinese authorities set up a twelve-man committee to tackle the "problem" of the Tibetan language. The invaders had found themselves trying to cope with a tongue that had no word for important things like lorries, airplanes, dynamos, or atom bombs, yet was choc-a-bloc with different terms for incomprehensibly subtle mental states.

Language reflects national preoccupations. In Tibet, a major pre-occupation—perhaps even *the* major preoccupation—has long been the results of meditation. Over several centuries, monks and nuns devoted entire lifetimes to stilling the mind and examining the nature of their inner processes.

Their motivation was, of course, religious. The Lord Buddha had instructed them to "seek out their own salvation with diligence" and showed them that mental discipline was the road to take. But as a by-product, their efforts led to an understanding of the human mind far more profound than anything Western psychology has yet produced.[19]

---

19. Depth psychology, notably of Jungian school, shares many insights with the Tibetan tradition, but while both seem to be moving in the same direction, Tibet had a head start of nearly three hundred years.

And some of them even developed strange powers in the process.

The idea that meditation can generate strange powers has a long provenance. The esoteric traditions of both Hindu India and Buddhist Tibet preserve very old legends of eighty-four near superhuman men and women who were prominent up to the eleventh century AD.[20] In Tibet, the most famous of them was the great eighth century Tantric master Padmasambhava, whose spiritual line of doctrine from guru to chela was believed to stretch intact until the time of the Chinese invasion . . . and perhaps beyond.

The powers exhibited by these people, according to one ancient text, fitted into an eightfold classification:

- Shrinking to the size of an atom.
- Becoming light enough to fly through the air (levitation).
- Becoming heavy.
- Touching faraway objects, even those as distant as the moon.
- The manifestation of irresistible will.
- Total control over body and mind.
- Dominion over the elements.
- The instant fulfillment of all desires.

All were taken literally, even the idea of shrinkage. A European visitor to a Tibetan monastery in the late 1940s was being shown around the gardens when he happened on a stone basin featuring a tiny pagoda surrounded by an exquisitely planted miniature landscape. When he expressed his admiration, his guide remarked that the basin was the home of the monastery's former Abbot, who had become immortal and shrunk to the size of a dragonfly, "but didn't come out much any more."

The remaining seven powers, with the possible exceptions of weather control and desire fulfillment, are all underpinned to some extent by Western observation and, in certain cases, scientific investigation.

---

20. The number eighty-four should not be taken literally—by convention it represents totality.

In Catholic countries, the power of levitation tends to be attributed to saints. St. Joseph of Cupertino and St. Teresa of Avila both suffered from the action of a mysterious force that lifted them into the air at inconvenient times. (St. Joseph often gave a little shriek when it happened, according to eyewitness reports.)

But the phenomenon is not confined to the holy. In 1906, a sixteen-year-old South African schoolgirl, Clara Germana Cele, levitated five feet off her bed during a seizure—and was promptly diagnosed as a case of demonic possession. The Scottish medium Daniel Dunglas Home demonstrated the same ability—this time under conscious control—when he astounded dinner guests at the home of Lord Adare by floating out through one third-story window and back in through another.

Interestingly, Home also demonstrated an ability to become preternaturally heavy. Although slimly built, he would sometimes appear to weigh so much that a circus strong man was unable to lift him. The phenomenon was also noted in a very different context by the British psychical researcher Kenneth Batcheldor in the 1960s. Batcheldor and a group of associates were investigating the Victorian séance-room art of table turning when they discovered that not only could levitations be persuaded to occur under controlled conditions, but there were times when the table appeared glued to the floor and could not be moved however many members of the party tried to lift it.

The ability to touch faraway objects is associated in the West with out-of-body experience (OOBE), during which certain people seem to leave their physical bodies and wander about like a ghost. The phenomenon is surprisingly common[21] and can often occur spontaneously at puberty. Orthodox psychologists tend to dismiss it as hallucination, while even psychical researchers, by and large, consider it a purely mental event—a sort of traveling clairvoyance. But a Latvian scientist named Karlis Osis has shown that there is more to it than that.

In a complicated experiment, a subject named Alex Tanous was required to leave his body to look at some target pictures placed in

---

21. Polls suggest as many as one person in four has experienced an OOBE at some stage of life.

such a way that they could only be viewed from a specially-constructed chamber. This chamber was not only shielded, but fitted with highly sensitive sensor plates and strain gauges. When Tanous reported (correctly) on the pictures he was viewing while out of the body, the gauges in the shielded chamber became active, suggesting the Tibetans are correct when they maintain that touch at a distance is entirely possible.

There are historians who would argue that 1930s Germany was subjected to a brutal example of "irresistible will" when Hitler came to power. Certainly the Fuhrer himself was convinced that will power of sufficient strength could influence even world events. But the Tibetan tradition of irresistible will may be closer to telepathic hypnosis than Hitler's criminal fantasies.

Reports of telepathic hypnosis date back to the eighteenth century when the inventor of modern induction techniques, the Marquis de Puységur, discovered that a subject named Madeline could be made to walk, sit, or pick up a specific object, all on purely mental commands. He was able to pass control to others, and when he did so, Madeline obeyed their mental orders as well.

In the late nineteenth century, a group of distinguished scientists engaged in an impromptu experiment that demonstrated that hypnotic *induction* by an act of will was also possible.

During a dinner party in 1886, the prominent French psychologist Pierre Janet was in the company of Frederick Myers, a founder of the British Society for Psychical Research, the psychologist Julian Ochorovicz, and a doctor from Le Havre called J. H. A. Gilbert. Over the port and cigars, Dr. Gilbert regaled his companions with an account of his hypnotic experiments with a subject named Léonie, who, he claimed, could be hypnotized by thought alone. The party decided to find out if it might be possible for Gilbert to hypnotize her, at a distance, there and then.

The experiment proved an outstanding success. Gilbert went to his study to concentrate. The others hurried to Léonie's home.

Moments later she emerged with her eyes tight shut, walking in a deep hypnotic trance.

Total control of body and mind by means of yoga practice is now well accepted in the West, even among the orthodox scientific community. Numerous tests using EEG (electroencephalograph) equipment have shown experienced yogis to be capable of changing their brainwave patterns—hence their mental states—at will. Body control includes slowing the heart rate, raising or lowering blood pressure, changing galvanic skin response, and even reducing the metabolism to such a level that it becomes possible to be buried alive for long periods of time without ill-effect.

Control of the elements and instant gratification of every wish are more controversial. Nonetheless, well-publicized "cloud-busting" experiments carried out in the latter half of the twentieth century and study of primitive rainmaking "magic" suggest that some form of mental weather control might actually be possible. There is, too, a strong tradition in the self-help community that "positive thinking" (that is, a specific mental state) can influence the outcome of events. This tradition receives some support from strong experimental evidence for psychokinesis, the ability to move objects using will power alone.

In Tibet, powers of this type are known as *grub-thob chen,* a term that absolutely equates with the Sanskrit *siddha.* The Buddha warned his followers about the development of siddhas, which he maintained were a barrier to spiritual progress. The warning is reinforced in Tibetan texts, which insist that the adept must go beyond such things in order to achieve spiritual freedom. A yogi who uses them for mundane gain will forever remain no more than a magician.

Despite the warnings, there were those who did just that. References in late Indian materials preserved in the monasteries of Tibet name a great sorcerer—Nagarjuna—who acquired magical power by means of spells and mysterious diagrams, then gained access to non-physical planes through diet and meditation. Some accounts claim he practiced alchemy and discovered the elixir of life.

Biographical accounts suggest Nagarjuna was born into a South India Brahman family sometime in the second century AD. Interestingly, he went beyond his magical practice when a great *bodhisattva*[22] introduced him to the profoundest teachings of Mahayana Buddhism. Thereafter, he became a noted philosopher and proclaimed the dharma[23] throughout India into his old age.

Tibet's greatest saint, Milarepa, was to follow essentially the same path.

Milarepa's birth name was Thopaga. He first saw the light of day near the border with Nepal in AD 1052, the son of a merchant. But at age seven, Thopaga lost his father. It was a devastating blow, and worse was to come. A greedy uncle promptly confiscated the family inheritance and turned Thopaga, his mother, and his sister out of their home.

Tibet is a hard country and Thopaga's mother found it difficult to survive with two small children. She managed, but not without building up a store of great bitterness and resentment toward her brother-in-law. The bitterness was shared by Thopaga, who eventually took to alcohol as a way of deadening his emotional pain. At age seventeen, he came home drunk one day, and when his disapproving mother chastised him, he promised to do anything she asked to make amends. Suddenly, all her pent-up resentment boiled over and she ordered him to find a sorcerer who would teach him the black magic needed for retribution on his uncle.

In the eleventh century, as in the twentieth, Tibetan belief in black magic was widespread and there were many individuals who claimed dark powers. One of them was a Lama named Yungtun-Trogyal[24] who had a fearsome reputation and was credited with the ability to raise storms and cause death at a distance. Thopaga asked to become his

---

22. An enlightened individual destined to become a Buddha.

23. Universal truth as proclaimed by the Lord Buddha.

24. This was evidently not the name he was born with; it translates as "wrathful and victorious teacher of evil."

pupil and the Lama agreed. After a lengthy period of apprenticeship, Thopaga was ready to take his revenge.

He waited until the wedding day of one of his cousins, a child of the uncle who had wronged him and his mother. Weddings in Tibet are cause for great celebration, with guests traveling many miles to attend. When everyone was assembled, Thopaga used techniques taught him by Yungtun-Trogyal to fill the house with vermin, then caused it to collapse. Thirty-five people died, but Thopaga spared his uncle and aunt "so that they might endure more suffering." Urged on by his mother, who was far from satisfied by the nightmare wedding, Thopaga conjured a hailstorm to destroy his uncle's crops, thus effectively ruining him.

Although Thopaga claimed to regret his actions afterward, he remained in Yungtun-Trogyal's service for many years and was approaching middle age before he finally decided to abandon the black arts. In a complete reversal of his former values, he apprenticed himself to a teacher named Marpa, the founder of the Kargyut-pa School of Tibetan Buddhism and a man widely regarded as a saint. Marpa refused to initiate his new pupil until he had atoned for his past sins, and for a six-year period subjected Thopaga to a rigorous regime of regular beatings and back-breaking tasks. One of these involved repeatedly building and tearing down a stone house.[25] It was not until Thopaga was forty-four that Marpa decided he had atoned for his sins and granted him the initiation he sought.

Thopaga then became as great a force for good as he had previously been for evil. On the death of his mother, which he foresaw in a dream, he vowed to devote his life to the ultimate spiritual goal. For a Buddhist like Thopaga, existence was governed by the Law of Karma, which, crudely stated, insists that present thoughts and actions absolutely determine your future state. Like virtually all Tibetans, he also believed implicitly in reincarnation. Against this background, the ultimate spiritual goal is liberation from the cycle of birth, death, and

---

25. This structure, in southern Tibet, was still standing in the twentieth century.

rebirth generated by karmic action. The liberated state, which involves experience of the mystical reality behind appearances, is called "Nirvana," although Tibetans often use the phrase "entering the Clear Light."

Although Nirvana is seen as a perfectly legitimate reward for spiritual labor, Thopaga not only vowed he would attempt to achieve it, but that if he did, he would renounce his personal liberation until all other sentient beings had achieved enlightenment as well. In other words, he determined to become a Buddha.[26]

In pursuit of his goal, Thopaga took up residence in the White Cave of the Horse's Tooth, a high mountain cavern where he was unlikely to be disturbed in his meditations. To survive the bitter cold, he became adept in the practice of *gtum-mo,* a mental discipline that generates great body heat.[27] Henceforth, he wore only a light cotton robe, known in Tibetan as a *repa,* which was to give him the name by which he is best known today: Milarepa.

In the high cavern, Milarepa's sole food was a soup made from nettles, which eventually gave his skin and hair a greenish tinge. Over the years he developed curious powers. He was able to leave his body at will and travel anywhere he wished, not only in this world, but in other levels of reality. He became a shapeshifter with the ability to metamorphose into various animals, birds, or even such things as a flame or a stream. There were claims that he could levitate.

As word of his abilities began to spread, Milarepa found that the remoteness of his cave no longer protected him from unwelcome visitors and he moved to an area near Mount Everest. There, a Lama who was jealous of Milarepa's fame sent him a gift of poisoned curds. Milarepa's psychism alerted him, but he explained to the messenger that while poison could no longer affect him, he was, at eighty-four,

---

26. Most Westerners assume there is only one Buddha, but this is not so. Prince Guatama, who founded the religion known as Buddhism some five hundred years before the birth of Christ, was only one in a chain of Buddhas past and present. The term means "Enlightened One."

27. And something we shall learn more about in the course of this book.

ready to leave this world anyway. He gathered together his disciples and preached to them for several days about karma and the nature of reality. Then he sank into *samadhi*, a trancelike state recognized as the prelude to Nirvana, and died.

According to a fifteenth-century biography of the saint, there were postmortem miracles. Milarepa revived his own corpse, then resurrected in a second body, which sang hymns amidst the flames of his funeral pyre before entering the Clear Light. Flowers rained down while comets streaked across the sky which formed itself into a mandala. When the flames of the pyre died there was no sign of Milarepa's bones or ashes—they had been carried off by *dakini* spirits.

Clearly, myth-making is at work in this biography. But that's not to say the entire story should be dismissed out of hand. Whatever about mandala skies, resurrected bodies, missing bones, and floral rain, the reports of strange powers are remarkably consistent. We've already seen that several of them are supported by Western scientific investigation. But the way such powers manifest in the West seems pale by comparison with Tibetan events. One typical European account of levitation, for example, describes how a Carmelite nun floated up a flight of stairs, then floated down again. Contrast that with Tibetan reports that Milarepa could eat, stand, lie, fly, and even sleep while levitating.

Is this a case of simple exaggeration? Or did Tibetan adepts gain more control over paranormal powers than the West has ever dreamed possible?

And if so, how did the Tibetans do it?

CHAPTER FIVE

ILLUSION AND REALITY

Madame Alexandra David-Neel, an intrepid French explorer who became the first European woman ever to be granted the title of Lama, brought back from Tibet the story of a spiritual practice so extraordinary that it must rank among the strangest in the world.

The practice, she claimed, was reserved for special initiates, noted by their gurus as having unusual potential for spiritual development. Typically it was applied only in a one-on-one situation, never when a group was being taught. What happened was this:

After the pupil had undergone several years of instruction, his guru would admit there was nothing more to be taught. The pupil must seek a more advanced master; and not necessarily a human master.

At this point, the guru suggested his pupil might evoke a *yidam*.

A yidam is a divine teacher who embodies an aspect of the enlightened mind and is thus held in especial esteem by Tibetans. There are four main types: peaceful, powerful, wrathful, and increasing. Each manifests in its specific form in order to combat particular types of negative forces. A creature of this type would, the guru claimed, be able to serve the pupil's needs throughout his life.

If the pupil agreed, it was usually with some trepidation. The evocation of a yidam was a perilous process and the yidam itself a dangerous entity. The whole thing had to be taken very seriously indeed.

As a preliminary, the pupil was set to study images of the deity. These were easily enough found since they illustrated many Tibetan scriptures. The creature itself was a fearsome-looking entity, but the study was prolonged and profound. Tibetan pictures of deities are stylized, and the smallest detail is often symbolic. The student made mental notes of everything about the yidam: skin coloring, clothing, ornaments, what the creature carried. All were important for the operation that was to follow.

The guru next instructed his pupil to find a suitable place for the evocation. It had to be isolated and remote since any interruption could prove disastrous, but it also had to be somewhere the pupil could stay for long periods of time. The guru suggested that his pupil find a cave, preferably at a high altitude, where no one was likely to visit.

When a suitable cave was found, the guru required his pupil to construct a *kylkhor,* a sort of magic circle designed to hold the yidam. Properly constructed, it ensured the deity could not attack his evoker.

The kylkhor itself took the form of a mandala, a complex symbolic diagram used in religious rites and as a focus of meditation. In Tibet it is believed to be a sacred area that functions as a collection point for universal forces and a receptacle for the gods.

Although mandalas may be painted on paper or cloth, fashioned in bronze, or even built in stone, the kylkhor used a different technique—the Tibetan art of sand painting.[28] In a process that took months to complete, the disciple first cleared and cleaned a space on the floor of his cave. He then set about memorizing the names, lengths, and positions of the primary lines that defined the basic structure.[29]

---

28. Called *dul-tson-kyil-khor*, the mandala circle of colored powders.

29. The lengths involved were relative. Mandalas may be constructed to various sizes, but their traditional proportions will always remain the same. To evoke a yidam, a very large kylkhor had to be designed.

The pupil next began to practice the technique of sand painting, an exacting process. Six primary colors are used—white, black, blue, red, yellow, and green—but four of these (blue, red, yellow, and green) come in dark, medium, and light shades, giving fourteen hues in all. The sands are stored in small, convenient pots and distributed by means of a tapered copper tube. The artist fills the tube with a particular color, closing off the narrow end with his finger. Then, holding the tube at an angle, he gently strokes it with a rod. The stroking motion causes the tube to vibrate and release a thin trickle of sand. With practice, Tibetan monks learn to release as little as a single grain at a time.

Once proficiency had been developed, the pupil set about constructing a full-scale kylkhor. First, he marked out the major axes and four baselines using chalk strings that had been blessed by his guru. Then, working from the center, he started the painstaking task of building up his picture.

A typical Tibetan mandala consists of an outer enclosure inside of which are one or more concentric circles, which in turn surround a square. Lines run from the center to the corners of the square, dividing it into four triangles. In the center five circles contain images of deities, with this pattern reflected in the middle of each triangle. There are four borders. The inmost depicts lotus leaves, the symbol of spiritual rebirth. Outside of that is a circle of eight graveyards, symbolizing aspects of cognition. Then comes a circle of diamonds, which stand for illumination. The outmost border is a ring of fire to bar the entry of ignorance.

Clearly, memorizing and reproducing a picture of this complexity requires an impressive proficiency in the art of visualization. But that's only the start. Although parts of this picture involve large areas of color, others comprise lines so fine they are no more than a grain or two of sand in width. The concentration needed to draw such lines is immense. Furthermore, as the pupil begins to stroke the tapered copper tube, it vibrates with a distinctive sound. The sound is hypnotic.

After a period of time working on a sand mandala, the artist passes into a state of trance.

Only when the pupil mastered the concentration, visualization, and trance state necessary to complete a sand mandala perfectly did his guru permit him to proceed with a yidam evocation.

Equipped with his newly developed skills, the pupil made his way to the high cave to begin the onerous task of constructing the kylkhor. When the kylkhor was finished—a job that took months—the guru came to inspect it. If was not satisfied, the entire diagram would have to be swept out and begun again.

Once the guru pronounced the kylkhor strong enough to hold the yidam, the invocation began. The main element was visualization. The pupil was required to seat himself outside the kylkhor and bend his mind toward imagining the deity so vividly that it appeared to be physically present.

How long a Tibetan student remained in his cave until he was able to see the yidam depended on personal talent and stamina. Some managed the hallucination sooner than others. But eventually the task was completed. When the image stabilized, the pupil hurried down the mountain to tell his master.

The guru congratulated him on his progress, but warned that simply evoking the deity to visible appearance—which is what he did with his feat of visualization—was not enough. If the entity was to become his teacher, he must be able to hear its words. Now he has to return to the cave and redouble his efforts until the yidam actually speaks to him. He must enter into a dialogue so he can seek its advice.

This aspect of the operation typically took less time than the initial visualization. The magician first heard the yidam's words in his mind, as if the entity was communicating telepathically. But with time, effort, and a great deal of concentration, the day came when the pupil heard the yidam in exactly the same way as he heard his guru.

When he reported this development, the guru again congratulated him, but told him that the operation was still not over. Now that he could hear the words of the deity, he must receive its blessing.

In Tibet, a blessing is an energy transfer accomplished by placing both hands on the communicant's forehead. The student now had to work in collaboration with the yidam until the creature solidified. When the blessing was given, the pupil had to be able to feel the deity's hands on his head. He must know the yidam was physically present, solid, and real.

Some pupils never managed it, just as some never managed to see the yidam in the first place. But the successful ones eventually reported back that the deity was now a living, breathing creature who has manifested fully in the cave.

At this point the guru told his pupil that while an end to his work was clearly in sight, the pupil had to achieve one more thing. While he had evoked a teacher of unsurpassed wisdom, the yidam was of little use to him while it remains locked in the kylkhor. It must be persuaded to emerge from the magic circle so that it could accompany the pupil, lending him its strength, powers, blessing, and wisdom throughout the rest of his life.

Tibetan pupils often balked at this development since they'd been culturally conditioned to view the yidam as dangerous as well as useful. But the guru was able to give reassurance. The fact that the yidam had favored the pupil with his conversation and his blessing indicated that the pupil was deemed worthy of the god's assistance. He need have no fear the yidam would ever harm him.

With this encouragement, the pupil returned to his cave and renewed his efforts. With time he succeeded. The yidam emerged from the kylkhor, took its place behind his left shoulder, and agreed to accompany him for the rest of his life.

Many pupils accepted this at face value and spent the remainder of their days guided by an invisible companion. They did so with the blessing of their gurus, who assured them they now had access to a master with the very highest degree of wisdom.

But a few developed doubts. They were unable to shake off the suspicion that the yidam was not a yidam at all, but rather a construction of their own mind, with no reality outside it. When the student returned to his guru to confess, he was immediately sent back to his cave with instructions to pray and meditate until such unworthy thoughts were rooted out.

Unfortunately, once doubt takes hold, it is very difficult to escape. Try as he might, the doubts remained.

"Do you not see the yidam?" the guru asked his pupil, who admitted that he did. "Do you not hear him, can you not touch him, do you not feel the energy of his blessing? Is he not as solid and real as the mountains around you?"

The student readily agreed to all this, yet he was now more convinced than ever that the yidam was a product of his mind.

And here the guru sprang his trap, for it was only the doubters who interested him. He told his pupil that the yidam really *was* no more than the product of his mind, but in that it was no different from the mountains, the cave, the sands that make up the kylkhor. No different, indeed, from anything else.

Everything in the physical world, without exception, was the product of the pupil's mind.

Although a masterful way of teaching, this esoteric con trick was not the only indication that devout Tibetans might view the world differently from you and me. In this they are heirs to a very ancient tradition. The curious notion that reality is actually an illusion first appeared in the Vedanta doctrines of (Hindu) India.

The fundamental premise of Vedanta is that there exists an eternal, all-embracing reality, without characteristics or attributes, which remains constant amidst the changing appearances of our universe. This reality is labeled "Brahman" and described as pure blissful conscious existence.

Brahman and our universe are related, but separate. The universe is an effect of Brahman in much the same way that heat is an effect of fire and inseparable from fire. But heat isn't the same as fire and the universe isn't the same as Brahman—the universe changes constantly; Brahman never changes at all.

The second great premise of Vedanta is that Brahman is knowable. As part of the manifest universe, your true nature (like that of everybody and everything else) is Brahman. If you'd like to know Brahman, you need to know yourself. But there's a catch. The self you have to know is not the ego-self—the Jean J. Jones or Sam S. Smith with which we normally identify. That "self" can't be known in its totality because it changes all the time. To reach Brahman within,[30] you must first cease to identify with the ego, which thinks of itself as separate and distinct from all other egos and, indeed, from the external universe. Identification with Brahman, however, reveals that all and everything is an essential unity.

The third of Vedanta's premises is that the purpose of life for every individual is to attain personal knowledge of Brahman. All of your activities should be directed to this end.

The plain fact that for most of us all of our activities are *not* directed to this end leads directly to the fourth and final fundamental tenet of Vedanta, which is that most people are bewildered by *maya.*

The term is often translated as *illusion,* but is, in fact, a little more subtle than that. Maya is the basis of both mind and matter, and, consequently, the "stuff" of which the universe is made. This means that as individuals we exist, think, and act within maya *and all we can normally perceive is maya.* Maya is a universe of changing values, full of contradictions like good and evil, and manifesting no absolutes at all. When the Hindu mystic Ramakrishna achieved enlightenment, he saw the universe as a game and his reaction was laughter, not through indifference but because he saw the reality behind the shadow.

Although not exactly fundamental to Buddhism, which concerns itself mainly with suffering and escape from the eternal wheel of reincarnation, there is a strong sympathy for the doctrine of maya in some, perhaps most, Buddhist schools. As such, it may have been

---

30. Called *Atman* in Vedanta. Strictly, the term *Brahman* is used only to describe external, transcendent Reality, while the same Reality when viewed as internal and immanent is called *Atman.* In this brief outline of Vedanta fundamentals, I've retained the term *Brahman* in both viewpoints for the sake of simplicity.

imported into Tibet in the seventh century, but even if not, its appearance was inevitable, given that fully a quarter of the population eventually turned toward religious practice. That practice centered on meditation and yoga, two roads that tend to circumvent the ego and lead to a realization of the essential Brahman-Atman beneath, whatever name happens to be given to the Ultimate Reality.

What we are talking about here is a Tibetan religion firmly rooted in mystical experience, and mystics of every tradition agree that the world is not what it seems. The goal of Vedanta is known as samadhi. Buddhists call the same superconscious state "Nirvana," or, in Tibet, the "Clear Light." Christians talk of the "Mystic Union." But in whichever country you stand, once the state is achieved, "the true nature of the object shines forth, not distorted by the mind of the perceiver."[31]

That the concept of maya really did take root in the Tibetan psyche is indicated by the Rite of Chöd, a much more widespread practice than the esoteric yidam evocation, but one equally designed to condition the mind to a new view of reality.

As described by Alexandra David-Neel,[32] this macabre ceremonial is so dangerous it can sometimes lead to madness, or even death. The rite itself is held anywhere that inspires terror—a haunted house or graveyard would be ideal, as would the site of a recent disaster. In Tibet, wild, desolate, barren environments tended to be chosen.

The initiate is equipped with a bell, *dorje,* a ritual dagger known as a *phurba,* a small *damaru* drum, and a human thighbone trumpet called a *kangling.* After some lengthy preliminaries aimed primarily at calming passions, he evokes a fearsome feminine deity who, if all goes well, emerges from the top of his head and faces him with a vicious sword in her hand.

The deity is required to cut off the initiate's head. As she does so—with a single swing of her sword—hungry ghouls begin to gather. The

---

31. The quote is from the great Hindu yogi and sage Patanjali.
32. In *Magic and Mystery in Tibet* (London: Souvenir Press, 1967).

goddess then embarks on a hideous process of butchery. She removes the initiates arms and legs, then flays the skin from his entire body. Next she cuts open his stomach and abdomen so that his intestines slide glistening onto the ground. The ghouls hurl themselves upon the feast.

The Rite of Chöd is deemed to be so important that some Lamas used to devote years to its practice, wandering into India, Nepal, Butan, and China in an effort to find new locations when they had exhausted suitable sites in their native Tibet. Tradition requires that it be carried through near 108 lakes and 108 cemeteries.

The fact that Chöd can be performed more than once makes it clear that the butchery does not *physically* involve the participant. The experience is, in fact, visionary, a trance nightmare voluntarily repeated again and again so that the initiate can feel the teeth of the ghouls ripping the flesh from his bones and later see himself a heap of miserable bones in a sea of mud.

As with the evocation of the yidam, the purpose of this ceremony is to convince the participant not only that the world is maya, but that the great illusion extends to his own body.

The concept of an illusionary universe arose in the West during the second half of the twentieth century, not as a philosophical speculation, but as a conclusion of physics. The atom was once believed to be the smallest possible piece of matter, but when it was successfully split and even smaller particles were discovered inside, a scientific search began to find the ultimate building block.

That search literally led nowhere. Physicists discovered smaller and smaller particles until, at the end of the road, they discovered that our entire manifest cosmos arose from a "quantum foam" of particles that continually appeared out of nowhere, existed momentarily, then disappeared again. It was the final confirmation of something known for several decades: our universe has no more than a *statistical* reality. It's unlikely that it will vanish before you read the end of this paragraph, but not impossible.

As you may have noticed, this surprising—not to say disturbing—discovery has no impact whatsoever on our daily lives. (Indeed, most people don't even know about it.) Much the same situation existed in Tibet when mystical investigation reached the same conclusion. The vast majority of Tibetans continued to live as if the world was real and solid.

But the foremost psychonauts of the monasteries, advanced yoga practitioners, thoughtful sorcerers, certain incarnate Lamas, and those mystics far advanced on the path of enlightenment all took note. Over many years their insights helped weave a rich tapestry of attitudes and doctrines that have permeated Tibetan religion, philosophy, mysticism, yoga, and esoteric practice ever since.

Part Two:

TIβETAN

MAGIC

CHAPTER SIX

LUNG-GOM-PA

According to tradition, *lung-gom-pa* runners were able to lighten their bodies and perhaps levitate in order to carry messages over vast distances across rough terrain. The runner whom Alexandra David-Neel saw did not levitate, but bounded along with a curious loping gait, almost like a bouncing ball, and appeared to be entranced.

Energy manipulation is also involved in the training of the lung-gom-pa runners reported by Alexandra David-Neel. She saw her first while traveling through the *Chang Thang,* a high, grassy region of Northern Tibet inhabited by only a few nomadic herdsmen. He appeared as no more than a spot on the distant horizon, but field glasses quickly resolved the image of a lone man moving with extraordinary speed. Madame David-Neel was warned by one of her party that she should not stop the runner or even speak to him, since this would cause the deity that possessed him to depart—something that would shake the man so badly he might die.

As the runner came closer, Madame David-Neel noted that his face was impassive and his eyes focused on a point in the sky. His left hand clutched the material of his robe while his right hand held a *phurba.* He was moving the ritual dagger almost as if it were a staff, although it was not remotely long enough to reach the ground. He did not run in the usual way, but bounded along in regular leaps as if he were a bouncing rubber ball. He did not appear to be aware of Madame David-Neel's party when he reached it.

Later, she saw another lung-gom-pa in even more curious circumstances. She was walking through a forest in Western Tibet with her adopted son Yongden when she came upon a naked man wrapped in heavy chains. He was sitting on a rock and seemed lost in meditation. But then he became aware of Madame David-Neel and her son, and ran off at astonishing speed. Yongden explained that lung-gom-pas sometimes wore such chains to weigh them down since their disciplines made their bodies so light they were in danger of floating away in the air.

In Kham, that rugged region of Tibet where guerrilla fighters gave so much trouble to the invading Chinese, Madame David-Neel met a lung-gom-pa in training. The man joined her party but was with them for a few days before she knew anything about his abilities. Then she saw him climbing a slope with extraordinary speed and agility, using the same bounding motion she had noticed in the other lung-gom-pas. When he reached her, the runner was not at all out of breath, but seemed barely conscious and incapable of speech. She realized at once that he was in trance. Later she learned that he had begun to study the techniques in a nearby monastery, but was now in search of a new teacher since his original guru had left the country.

It transpired that the trance state Madame David-Neel witnessed had come on the man spontaneously, triggered by a desire for grilled meat. Although the training methods of a lung-gom-pa were secret, she managed to extract the information that he had been told to look steadily at a starry sky as part of his technique. She also learned that sunset or clear nights were the best times to practice lung-gom-pa running.

The man was headed for Shalu Gompa Monastery, a center specializing in lung-gom-pa training. According to a tradition dating back to the fourteenth century, the techniques had been developed when a swift runner was needed to collect various demons scattered around the country. The demons were then propitiated in a powerful and important religious ceremony commemorated at twelve-year intervals right up to the Chinese invasion. A runner, called a *maheke-tang*, was traditionally elected from one of two monasteries to play the part of the demon-wrangler. His training, isolated in total darkness, took three years and three months to complete.

It is known that maheketang training—generally accepted to be similar to that of a lung-gom-pa—involved breathing exercises and a very curious form of yoga apparently designed to lighten the body. This yoga, reminiscent of a practice that forms part of the modern Transcendental Meditation movement, consists of jumping while cross-legged following a series of deep in-breaths. Since the hands are not used, the knack seems to be related to violent movement of the buttock and/or thigh muscles. But however managed, adepts eventually train themselves to jump to remarkable heights. The legend in Tibet was that after years of practice, the body became so light that it was possible to sit on an ear of barley without bending the stalk. In other words, the jumping yoga eventually led to levitation.

The "lung" of lung-gom-pa is an alternative transliteration of the term rlung, which describes the energies we examined in chapter 2— a clue to the essential nature of lung-gom-pa training. Indeed, it is known that "lung-gom" is an umbrella term for a series of practices designed to generate physical or spiritual results, of which trance running is only one example. It seems clear that the thrust of the training is an attempt to influence the body's subtle energy system.

Madame David-Neel was so intrigued by what she saw of lung-gom-pa that she made a comprehensive investigation into the methods behind it. She discovered that initial preparation required several years of practice in yoga breathing, and only when proficiency was obtained would a lung-gom-pa guru permit a pupil to attempt the actual running. At this point, however, the pupil was given a mantra that was to be recited mentally both in time with the breathing and in time with every step taken.

The running was initially practiced only on clear nights in a fairly featureless, flat environment. This meant that the pupil could be assigned a particular star as a focus for his gaze while running. It also meant that there were few obstacles to negotiate while he was developing his proficiency. Madame David-Neel records[33] that some runners would stop when their star dropped below the horizon, but others internalized the vision and could continue their journey regardless.

When you put all this information together, it becomes possible to make an intelligent guess about what is going on here. Both yoga breathing and sound have an influence on the rlung energies. While the breath control would almost certainly have followed the traditional techniques developed to strengthen the energy system and promote good health, it is likely that the guru would have chosen a mantra that contained sounds best suited to the specific chakra system of the pupil. Although eventually internalized, the mantra would initially have been spoken aloud and the chakras stimulated accordingly.

We shall examine mantras in more detail later, but for the moment it is enough to point out that they are more than the sounds they contain. A suitable mantra runs to a particular rhythm—and rhythm is hypnotic. But rhythm is not the only hypnotic element to be seen in lung-gom-pa training.

A common preliminary to hypnotic induction is the requirement for your subject to fix his or her attention on a particular spot above eye level. This quickly has the effect of tiring the eyes and inducing a sensation of relaxation and sleepiness, which can easily be transformed into trance in suitable subjects. Exactly the same process is evident in the requirement for the lung-gom-pa runner to fix his gaze on a star.

Another aid to hypnotic induction is the flat, featureless environment. Although this is undoubtedly a safety feature as well, the boredom of running through such an environment is hypnotic in itself. When motorways were first introduced in Europe and Britain, their designers followed the logic of the shortest distance by making them as straight as possible. But there were so many instances of drivers

---

33. In *Magic and Mystery in Tibet* (London: Souvenir Press, 1967).

"falling asleep" behind the wheel that artificial curves had to be added. Many drivers did not, in fact, fall asleep at all. They fell into a hypnotic trance.

The fixation of the gaze, the uninteresting environment, the rhythm of the internalized mantra synchronized with rhythmic breathing and leg movement, all combine to become a powerful hypnotic induction. Like early motorway users, the runner drops quickly into trance.

Trance of this type has several interesting implications. As hypnotists have demonstrated again and again, entranced subjects are capable of feats of strength and endurance far beyond anything they might achieve in their waking state. Powers of visualization increase so that the image of the star replaces the actuality and allows the runner to continue his progress during daylight hours. So, interestingly, do powers of memory. In Tibet, lung-gom-pa runners were traditionally used as message carriers, yet none of the descriptions in David-Neel and elsewhere mention that they carry scrolls, books, or other texts. The messages, however complex, seem to have been stored in the runner's mind.

Thus, the typical lung-gom-pa is a trance runner with a heightened energy system and considerable experience in breath control—three elements that go a long way toward explaining the prodigious feats of speed and endurance that have been reported. But is levitation also a possibility? Many Tibetan texts claim that, in time, a lung-gom-pa may become so proficient that his feet no longer touch the ground.

The demonstrations of "hypnotic" levitation that feature in so many stage conjuring acts are achieved by mechanical means, not trance. But trance can certainly leave you with the subjective impression that your body is lighter—although it is true to say that a subjective impression of heaviness is just as likely. If levitation really is a factor in lung-gom-pa running, it is more likely to come about through sonic chanting or some other manipulation of the energy system than simple trance.

Although few Westerners are prepared for the commitment involved in years of training—and indeed trance running through city streets might prove a great deal more dangerous than it ever did on the Tibetan plateau—it is perfectly possible to experience some elements of lung-gom-pa for yourself in your local gym.

First, check out your baseline performance on one of the mechanical stamina trainers like the treadmill or fixed bicycle. Then, having rested, repeat the experiment while synchronizing your movements with an inner mantra—you might like to try the famous *om mani padme him*, but almost any rhythmic form of words will do. You will find that your stamina improves. If you can manage to synchronize your breathing, too, the improvement can be quite dramatic. Even the simple act of closing your eyes and visualizing a star above and before you can make a difference.

CHAPTER SEVEN

GTUM-MO

Over the years, travelers' tales filtered out of Tibet about sorcerers who had conquered the cold to such a degree that they could walk naked above the snowline without fear of frostbite or hyperthermia, indeed without any particular discomfort at all. One (not altogether reliable) source claimed to have witnessed Himalayan competitions, organized rather like an English village fair, at which adepts in the art sat attempting to melt snow with their bottoms. The one to produce the largest pond of melt-water was supposedly given a prize.

Unlikely though such stories sound, it transpired that certain Tibetans really had developed the art of generating an extraordinary degree of body heat—quite enough to endure conditions that would kill a normal person. The techniques that allowed them to do so, possibly modifications of obscure Indian yogas, were gathered under the name *gtum-mo* (pronounced "tummo").

Gtum-mo adepts were given the title *repas* in Tibet (as in Milarepa) after the thin cotton robe they wore in all weathers. Typically, the student of gtum-mo received his repa only after undertaking a rigorous test. Stripped naked, he was wrapped in a blanket that had been soaked in a freezing mountain stream and required to dry it thoroughly using only his own body heat. When this blanket was dry, he was immediately required to dry another, then a third. Only after the third blanket was he pronounced proficient in his art.

The term *gtum-mo* actually means heat or warmth, but only in the special sense of psychic heat. Tibetans recognize three types:

1. The gtum-mo that arises spontaneously during ecstatic religious experience.
2. Mystic gtum-mo, which is the fire of bliss itself.
3. Esoteric gtum-mo, which keeps the adept physically warm.

The third type of gtum-mo—the one with which we are concerned here—is related to the subtle fire that warms the seminal fluid in a man and is the source of its energy (called *shugs* in Tibet). When the warmth is heightened, the energy runs throughout the rtsa channels.

Clearly, gtum-mo is not an exclusively masculine prerogative since Madame David-Neel was able to practice it, so the references to seminal fluid relate more to a male bias in Tibetan esoteric practice than to any technical reality. What seems to be important here is the energy generated at the sexual center, the base chakra Wheel of the Preservation of Happiness. This energy is, of course, common to both men and women.

Gtum-mo initiation is essentially an empowerment—the passing of *angkur* (the ability to do it) from guru to chela, a little like the pho-wa transference we examined earlier. But recognition only comes after a lengthy period of training, so the likelihood is that the chela really does most of the work and the initiation marks a particular level attained.

In Tibet, trainees were cautioned never to practice inside a house or near other people since "foul air" and "negative vibrations" could hinder progress or even cause harm. Here again is an indication that the practice involved energy manipulation at a subtle level.

Once initiated, the adept was required to renounce the use of fur or wool clothing and never warm himself at a fire. Like many formalized traditions, this one had practical roots. The practice of gtum-mo requires constant reinforcement. As an athlete who ceases to train soon loses his edge, so a gtum-mo adept will eventually lose his abilities if he relies too much on external heat sources or warm clothes.

The art of gtum-mo requires a considerable investment of time. Traditional training takes three years, three months, and three days.

There are five preliminary exercises designed to prepare you for the raising of gtum-mo. All involve visualization, and one involves something similar to prayer. They are based on the idea that visualization can influence the flow of energy throughout the subtle channels of the body.

Exercise One

The first exercise begins with a particular form of prayer believed to lead to a mystical communion with your root guru. Several variations of the prayer exist (one is given in chapter 3 of the present work). When the prayer is completed, you are required to visualize yourself as the naked, virginal sixteen-year-old Vajra-Dakini, the divinity we met in the same chapter, where you will find a full description of her appearance.[34]

In your initial visualization, you should see yourself in the form of this goddess, and about your own size. But once the image is established, you should imagine yourself growing to the size of a house, then the size of a hill. Continue to grow until your goddess form is large enough to encompass the entire universe, and spend a little time in contemplation of this state.

Next, you must gradually reduce in size, step by step, little by little, until you are no larger than a mustard seed.[35] Then you should shrink the imaginal visualization even farther, so that it is microscopic in extent, yet retains all its fine detail. Contemplate yourself in this minuscule state as well.

---

34. While the external form of the goddess is as given, you should simultaneously visualize yourself internally as empty, like a balloon.

35. The original texts use the Sanskrit term *til*, a tiny seed of an Indian plant. I've taken the liberty of altering this to something with which Western readers might be more familiar.

Exercise Two

The second exercise builds on the first in that you begin by imagining yourself as the normal-sized Vajra-Yogini goddess. But having done this, you should now concentrate on visualizing the *dbu-ma* energy channel that runs down the center of your body. It should be seen as straight, hollow, about the size of an arrow shaft, and a bright, almost luminous, red.

As before, you are required to expand the visualization until the channel becomes the size of a walking staff, then a pillar, a house, a hill, and finally large enough to contain the whole of the universe. In this form, the channel pervades the whole of your body, right through to the fingertips, although in its natural state it does nothing of the sort.

Again, as you did in the first exercise, shrink your visualized image until the hollow channel is no more than one one-hundredth the thickness of a human hair.

Exercise Three

Your third exercise involves a special posture and breathing sequence preliminary to the visualization exercises. The recommended posture is called the Buddha or Dorje Posture in Tibet, and corresponds to the Lotus Pose of Hatha Yoga. Sit on the floor with your legs crossed so that your feet rest on your thighs, the soles turned upward. Your right leg should be on top.

This posture is almost impossible for Westerners without extensive yoga training, and seems to have been tricky enough for Tibetans since an easier alternative is given. This is the Siddha Posture—the Perfect Pose of Hatha Yoga—in which your legs are crossed so that the left heel presses into the perineum while the right foot nestles into the fold of the left leg. The use of a meditation band is recommended. This is a sturdy strip of material roughly four times the circumference of your head that can be fastened in a loop around the back of the neck and underneath your knees so that it holds your basic posture in place. A well-stuffed meditation cushion about twenty-two inches square and four finger-widths thick is also permitted.

Whichever posture is adopted, you should place your hands in your lap at a level just below your navel with the back bend of the wrists pressed against your thighs. Your thumb, forefinger, and little finger should be extended, the other two bent into the palm. Straighten your spine and expand your diaphragm as far as it will go. Press your chin against your throat, place your tongue against the roof of your mouth, and fix your eyes on the tip of your nose, the horizon, or the sky.

Once in position, exhale completely to rid your lungs of stale air. Repeat this three times, then inhale as fully as possible and raise your diaphragm slightly so that your chest takes on the appearance of a pot. Hold your breath as long as you can without undue strain.

As you breathe out, imagine that five-color rays emerge from every pore of your body to fill the entire world. The colors, which equate to the elements, are blue, green, red, white, and yellow—symbolizing, respectively, ether, air, fire, water, and earth. On the inbreath, imagine these rays returning through the pores to fill your body with multicolored light. Repeat the exercise seven times.

Next, imagine that each ray changes into a five-color version of the syllable *hum*. This is obviously a great deal easier for someone familiar with the Tibetan alphabet than it is for the majority of Westerners, but a representation of the syllable is shown below for guidance. On your out-breath, visualize the world as filled with these five-color *hum* syllables and listen to the sound they make. On the in-breath, imagine the syllables entering and filling your body. Repeat this breathing/visualization sequence seven times.

hum

Now, on the out-breath, imagine that the *hum* syllables become mustard-seed sized representations of angry deities. As a monk in Tibet, you would be surrounded by various representations of Wrathful Deities, since these have found their way into many religious texts and much religious art. It may be that you will wish to search out and study some of these images for yourself before embarking on this segment of the exercises, but it is an equally valid approach to imagine the deities creatively, based on the following description:

First, make no attempt to duplicate the multiheaded and many-armed deities found in some of the Far Eastern pantheons—the gods and goddesses you visualize should have only the requisite single face and two hands. The right hand holds aloft a dorje (see illustration), while the left is held against the heart. Like the rays, each deity is five-colored. Their right legs are bent, the left legs held tense. They should be seen as very fierce, angry, and menacing.

Dorje

Just as before, imagine that on the out-breath the visualized deities go out to fill the world, while on the in-breath they return to fill your body. Again, repeat the sequence seven times.

The next step represents a critical stage in the exercise. You are required to imagine that every pore of your body is inhabited by one of these tiny deities with his face turned outward. The result of this visualization, when performed correctly, is that you see yourself as having grown a second protective skin composed of fierce and angry deities, which functions rather like a suit of chain mail armor.

Exercise Four

You begin the fourth preliminary exercise by visualizing the hollow ro-ma and rkyang-ma channels on either side of the midline. Next you should imagine the five vowels of the alphabet within the left channel and the twenty-one consonants in the right channel.[36] Each letter should have a fine outline and be seen as the color red. Imagine them arranged in a vertical line, one above the other. Establish a breathing routine that alternates left and right nostrils—you may have to close off the alternate nostril with thumb or forefinger to do this—then visualize the letters streaming out with your out-breath, one after another. On the in-breath, imagine them returning, but entering your body through your penis or vagina. The Tibetan texts use a particularly pleasing simile for this process when they talk of the letters following each other "like fairy fires."[37]

Exercise Five

The final preliminary exercise requires you to visualize your root guru seated cross-legged in your heart chakra with the chain of gurus imagined in ascending order of importance, one above the head of the other in a vertical line along your central energy channel. When the visualization is firmly in place, use the following prayer:

> *Grant me your inspiration, O gurus, that my mind may develop the four powers.*
> *Grant me your inspiration that everything visible may appear to me in the form of deities.*
> *Grant me your inspiration that the vital force may enter the center channel.*

---

36. Original Tibetan texts state that you should imagine one vowel and one consonant in the left and right channels, respectively, but subsequent instructions make it clear that the whole alphabet is to be used.

37. For those unfamiliar with Tibetan, it may be worth experimenting with the English alphabet. Preliminary investigation suggests it may work equally well.

Grant me your inspiration that the blissful warmth of gtum-mo may flare up.

Grant me your inspiration that the illusory bodily may be transformed.

Grant me your inspiration that the pure body of reality may appear.

Grant me your inspiration that the illusion of dreams may be dispelled.

Grant me your inspiration that the clear light may be recognized as existing within me.

Grant may your inspiration that paradise maybe attained through the practice of pho-wa.

Grant me your inspiration that Buddhahood may be attained in this lifetime.

Grant me your inspiration that the Clear Light may be attained.

When the prayer is finished, imagine the entire chain of gurus merging into the body of the root guru, which in turn merges into the essence of bliss. Allow this experience of bliss to fill your body.

With the preliminaries complete, you can now move on to the actual generation of psychic heat. Begin by adopting either the Buddha or Siddhi postures described in the third preliminary exercise. Keep your spine straight, expand your diaphragm, and drop your chin on to your chest. Place your tongue against the roof of your mouth. Fix your eyes are on the tip of your nose. Now link your thought processes with your breathing in order to take control of your mind.

Like most Eastern yoga forms, this one links breath control with mind control and involves learning a complex breathing sequence. You begin with what the texts call "calm breathing."

Close off your left nostril with your forefinger so that you are breathing only through the right nostril.

Turn your head slowly from right to left while inhaling and exhaling three times through the right nostril.

Now close off your right nostril and inhale/exhale three times while moving your head slowly from left to right.

Finally, with your head steady and looking straight ahead, inhale/exhale three times through both nostrils.

This sequence of nine breaths is known as "bellows breathing" and should be repeated three times. For the first of these three sequences, you should breathe so gently that the breaths are scarcely perceptible. For the second, you need to breathe more strongly, while for the third, your breath should empty the lungs completely on an exhalation and fill them totally on an inhalation. (You will need to make use of your abdominal muscles to achieve this.)

When you have completed the full sequence of bellows breathing, move on to what is known as the "four combined breathing." For this, you should bend your head forward so that your neck takes on the shape of a hook. Now draw in air through both nostrils from a distance of about sixteen finger-widths without making a sound.[38]

The air from this silent in-breath should reach the bottom of your lungs. Contract your diaphragm to raise the thorax so that your chest puffs out.

You will find that this potlike expansion of your chest quickly becomes difficult to sustain. When it does, you are instructed to draw in a series of short breaths using muscular action to direct these inhalations to right and left lungs, respectively, so that pressure is equalized in both lungs. Although easy to describe, this is less easy to do and may take practice.

Once you have reached your limit in the process of equalization, breathe out through both nostrils gently at first, then with greater force, then gently again, all on a single exhalation. This process is described as "shooting the breath forth like an arrow." When you try it, you will understand why.

Next comes a sequence called "violent breathing," which is broken down into five separate techniques.

---

38. This is not a particularly logical instruction, but it communicates well what is needed.

Technique One

The first of these is simply emptying the lungs completely, then slowly refilling them to their fullest extent. The emphasis is on *slowly*. The stated purpose of the exercise is to prevent a rebound effect that is the natural reaction to emptying the lungs—a tendency to take quick, short breaths.

Technique Two

The second technique is described[39] as the "art of in-breathing to cause the air to enter into all its natural channels." No further explanation is given in the texts, but a commentary by the distinguished British scholar W. Y. Evans-Wentz suggests that this simply means working to make the first violent breathing exercise habitual, although I suspect that what's really needed is the visualization of cosmic energy entering the various channels in time with the breath.

Technique Three

The third technique is breath retention, which permits a fuller extraction of the vital energy from the air. Practice will, of course, enable you to hold your breath for increasingly long periods of time, but it is important to do so without strain. It is also important to be conscious of the purpose of the exercise—the extraction of vital energy from the retained air. Here, too, visualization will be of benefit.

Technique Four

Technique Four seeks mastery over the breathing process so that the vital energy extracted from the air enters the various rtsa channels. This process, which reflects exercises used in the Western Esoteric Tradition, can be aided by visualization—imagine the light gently spreading throughout your entire body and permeating every pore.

---

39. In *Tibetan Yoga and Secret Doctrines*, by W. Y. Evans-Wentz (London: Oxford University Press, 1969).

Technique Five

The final technique of the sequence seeks to mingle the internalized life force with the great reservoir of cosmic energy all around you. This is referred to as the "art of relaxing the breathing," a name that suggests the process involves an out-breath.

The third and final part of the gtum-mo process involves the manipulation of mental images.

The first of these is one with which you are already familiar from the preliminary exercises—the image of the Vajra-Yogini. But now, instead of imagining yourself as this deity, you should create an image of the goddess standing normal human size before you. This image becomes your contact point with the universal energy.

Next, visualize the central dbu-ma channel with its four major chakras flanked by the ro-ma and rkyang-ma channels on the right and left, respectively. Begin by visualizing the hollow, perpendicular central channel, red in color but transparent and bright. This channel, you will recall, begins at the crown of the head and ends four finger-widths below the navel. Now visualize the two peripheral channels that extend over the top of the brain and pass through the openings of the nostrils to travel downward, flanking the central channel until they curve inward to join it at the bottom.

With the three channels clearly visualized, you should add the chakras to your image. The crown chakra should be visualized as radiating thirty-two "energy spokes"—minor rtsa channels—downward into the head. These are met by sixteen more that radiate upward from the throat center. Eight channels radiate down from the heart center, while sixty-four radiate up from the navel center. The texts suggest that these visualizations are somewhat like the spokes of chariot wheels on the axis of the median channel, but the picture is very approximate.

Now comes what is understood as the core visualization of gtum-m. According to the ancient texts, the secret of producing psychic heat lies in the use of one half of the letter *A*—in other words, a visualized shape like one half of the Tibetan *A* will influence the energy system.

The Tibetan letter *A* is a symbol written like this:

ཨ་

Half of this symbol must be either

ཅ

or possibly

ༀ་

According to Evans-Wentz, the former shape, somewhat like the Arabic numeral 3, is used by Tibetan mystics. The shape should be visualized at the point where the three major channels meet, four finger-widths below the navel. See it outlined hair-thin, reddish brown in color, and hot to the touch, floating and undulating. As it moves, the shape makes a sound like the spluttering of a lighted taper.

Next visualize the Tibetan letter *ham* on the median channel within the crown chakra at the top of your head. The letter, which looks like this, ཧྃ་, should be visualized as white in color with a single drop of nectar forming on the "tail" at the bottom.

Draw in a breath to bring the life energy into the left and right channels and see them expand in your mind's eye, as if they were blown up by the air. Watch the vital force enter the middle channel and travel down to reach the visualized ཅ, which fills out from its original outline until it becomes a fully-shaped red form. As you breathe out, imagine that the air leaves the median channel in a bluish stream.

Continue this sequence of breathing and visualization until it is well established—that is, until it becomes so easy the various elements seem to occur of their own accord—then change the sequence slightly so that on the in-breath a tiny, pointed flame, no more than half a finger-width long, flares up from the outlined ཅ. The flame should be upright, bright red in color, and transparent. It should also flicker in such a way that it appears to be spinning. Now, with each in-breath, imagine that the flame rises half a finger-width higher so that by the time you complete eight breathing cycles, it reaches the navel chakra. Two cycles later, the flame will have extended into every petal of this center.

Over the next ten breath cycles, the imaginal fire thus kindled moves down to the lower part of your body, filling your lower abdomen, legs, feet, and toes.

In ten further breath cycles, it moves upward in stages, filling your body as far as the heart chakra.

Over the next ten cycles, it reaches the throat chakra, then, with ten more breaths, it reaches the Thousand-Petaled Lotus of the crown chakra at the top of your head.

You will recall that you have already established the letter *ham* ($\overset{\circ}{\xi}$) within this center. As the imaginal fire reaches this chakra, it slowly dissolves the symbol over the next ten breath cycles into a pearlescent "moon fluid," which spreads to fill the entire lotus.

This moon fluid is the key to the gtum-mo effect. Watch in your mind's eye as it overflows from the Thousand-Petaled Lotus to fill throat, heart, and navel chakras, then the entire body, each taking ten-breath cycles.

The overall sequence of 108 breath cycles constitutes a single gtum-mo course. To become proficient, you need to repeat six courses over each twenty-four hour period in the early stage of your training, stopping only for food and sleep. However, the deep breathing aspect of this yoga has the effect of increasing your lung capacity—something that will be quite noticeable after about a month. With increased lung capacity, you will naturally increase your intake of the universal life force. Once this happens, you should reduce the number of repetitions to four.

With this groundwork completed, you can trigger the gtum-mo heat in one of three ways. By far the simplest is the use of breathing: push the inhaled air to the bottom of your lungs, then contract your diaphragm to expand the chest. The two remaining methods are as follows:

1. While seated in a simple cross-legged position, grasp the underneath of your thighs with your hands. Use your stomach muscles to circle the stomach three times from right to left and three times from left to right. Churn the stomach vigorously by rippling the muscles from top to bottom, then shake the body like a dog that has just come out of the water. While you are doing so, raise yourself a little on your crossed legs, then drop back again onto your cushion—in effect bouncing a little off the floor. Repeat this whole exercise three times, ending with a more vigorous bounce.

2. Visualize yourself as the Vajra-Yogini with the three main channels, the chakras, and the ই symbol all visible. Imagine blazing suns in the palms of your hands and the soles of your feet. Bring your hands together and your feet together so that the suns meet. Visualize another sun at the junction of the main channels four finger-widths below the navel. Now rub together the suns in the palms of your hands and the soles of your feet. When you do so, fire will flare up to strike the sun below the navel, then the ই symbol and will go on to permeate your whole body.[40] On your next out-breath, visualize the psychic heat going out to fill the whole world.

The ancient texts promise that if you perform twenty-one vigorous bounces while engaging in the visualization sequence and repeat the exercise for seven days, you will be able to endure almost any degree of cold while wearing only the thin cotton repa robe.

---

40. You can experience a curious phenomenon at this point in that the fire will often spring up before your mental eye without your actually willing it—something that seems to support Tibetan ideas of a close relationship between the energy system and the visual imagination.

CHAPTER EIGHT

GTUM-MO OF THE SPIRIT

The experience of a gtumo-mo goes far beyond this simple stimulation of body heat. Tibetans recognize two different types, one classified as normal, the other supernatural.

If, for example, you store the cosmic energy in the psychic centers, heat is produced at first, but an experience of bliss follows. The mind then assumes its natural state of tranquility and thoughts stop automatically. This is followed by visionary experiences, including that of light and something resembling the void of a cloudless sky.

The process that leads to these results is well charted. You delay the out-breath by a conscious effort, and this stores energy in the chakras.

By retaining the vital force in this way, the waves of psychic heat are made stable. This has at tranquilizing effect both on the mind and on the stored energy. As tranquility is achieved, heat is produced.

The effect of the heat is to stimulate the opening of the psychic channels into which the energy carries the moon fluid. At first the experience is negative—the channels become painful, as do the seminal vesicles in a man.[41] But this is only a preliminary to a much more

---

41. Tibetan texts make it quite clear that the "moon fluid" is associated with semen, but it is equally clear that semen and moon fluid are not one and the same thing.

pleasant state. As the channels become rejuvenated by the inflow of energies, an experience of bliss follows.

The transformative effect of the state enables you to regard the whole of nature as joyful. The incessant internal chatter of thought that is the normal condition for most of us is looked on by Tibetan mystics as a type of poison, which is neutralized in the course of gtum-mo practice. Once this has done, the mind falls into its natural state of tranquility, the state of samadhi, which is a preliminary to Nirvana.

Although the mind is calm and the practitioner has entered into something equivalent to a trance state, consciousness is not lost. There is an awareness of external reality, although much of its phenomena takes on the appearance of a mirage. Some texts advise the practitioner to pay attention to any omens that may arise, although he is simultaneously warned not to go looking for them.

There is a widespread belief that as you become adept in the techniques of gtum-mo, you will become immune to disease and the physical deterioration caused by ageing.

Supernatural, or at least super normal, effects are also expected to occur. Visions of red, white, blue, pink, and yellow auras will typically appear and your body itself might develop a halo affect. The halo is taken as a visible sign of certain changes within the body—increased strength, suppleness, immunity to fire, and lightness. In extreme cases, the body is believed to become transparent and, eventually, is transmuted into pure light invisible to other people.

Tibetans believe the action of *karma* is controlled by certain chakra centers.[42] The Wheel of Transformation at the navel houses the principle that causes karmic debts to be translated into karmic actions. The Wheel of Phenomena at the heart contains the principle that causes karmic results to emerge. The throat center (Wheel of Enjoyment) has the latent ability to increase karmic propensities. The

---

42. Karma is the sum of a person's actions in previous lives, viewed as deciding his or her fate in future existences.

Wheel of Bliss crown chakra has the potential to free the individual from karmic debt.

As the moon fluid moves upward through these centers, the karmic principles are stimulated and the upper end of the midline channel begins to vibrate uncontrollably. This, in turn, creates a brand-new psychical organ that protrudes (invisibly) through the crown of the head and allows the manifestation of *bodhic* consciousness.[43] During gtum-mo practice, this occurs when the new organ fills with moon fluid, setting up a vigorous energy circuit in which transmuted sexual energy flows upward from the base chakra to the crown, while a second energy, reddish in color, flows down from the crown to permeate every cell of the body.

---

43. Interestingly, many images of the Lord Buddha show a protuberance in this area, although it is often symbolized as an ornamental headdress.

CHAPTER NINE

TIBETAN TULPAS

Tibetan pursuit of mystical states and magical effects led to some remarkable discoveries, none more intriguing than the amazing power of the imagination. In earlier chapters, we saw how visualization can influence the body's energy system and, in doing so, change consciousness to varying degrees until the Clear Light of Nirvana is attained.[44]

But somewhere on that great inner journey, Tibetans discovered that the human mind is not what we believe it to be, that the boundary between subjective and objective is essentially meaningless, and that thoughts are things with a reality that matches trees and stones . . . or even living creatures.

There are hints of similar conclusions in Western psychology, particularly the Jungian school. Carl Jung talked cautiously about the "objective psyche" and "collective unconscious," which contained elements that were not the result of individual experience and consequently could not be seen as subjective constructs. In his investigation of mediumistic phenomena, he theorized about "semi-automatous complexes," defined as constellations of psychic contents that behaved

---

44. Personal insight into this process may be what prompted the poet and visionary William Blake to remark that "imagination is proof of the Divine."

as personalities in their own right and were beyond the control of the individual who experienced them.[45] It is probably true to say that a majority of Western psychologists (of whatever school) also believe the voices heard by Spiritualist mediums are, at best, dramatized aspects of their own unconscious.

There is no doubt at all that the human mind is perfectly capable of dramatizing aspects of its own unconscious—novelists and playwrights do it all the time. Indeed, authors have frequently remarked on the propensity of fictional characters to take on a life of their own and behave in ways that are often inconvenient to the plot. But Tibetan mystical psychology goes further. It theorizes that with sufficient concentration and effort, thought-forms may take on physical substance (of a sort) and achieve a degree of reality that renders them visible to others.

It was the ubiquitous Madame Alexandra David-Neel who brought news of that last discovery out of Tibet. One evening she was resting in her high Himalayan camp when a scurry of activity alerted her to the appearance of an unexpected visitor. Although he had stumbled on the camp quite accidentally, it transpired that Madame David-Neel knew him. He was a well-known artist from Lhasa she had met years before.

The man had changed alarmingly. He looked ill—she thought he might be feverish—and seemed ill-at-ease, even jumpy. But that was not what concerned Madam David-Neel. Looming over the man was a monstrously large, shadowy presence, perfectly visible, but no more solid than a curl of incense smoke. From her Buddhist studies, she recognized the figure as one of the gods in the Tibetan pantheon. It seemed to follow the artist everywhere he went.

She began to question him. Tibetan artists tend to paint religious themes, and since they last met, he had formed a special devotion to a

---

45. In later life, however, Jung decided that "the spirit hypothesis best fitted mediumistic phenomena." In other words, mediums really were in contact with spirits and not simply aspects of their own deep mind.

particular deity. He studied the god for several months and, using scriptural references, painted its picture again and again. Gradually, it came to fill his daily meditations and his daily thoughts. Eventually he decided to devote his life to it. Madame David-Neel quickly realized that the object of his devotions was the same shadowy figure that now followed him.

As a European—Madame David-Neel was born in France—she was reluctant to believe that an actual god had entered her camp. As an initiate Lama, she was familiar with Tibetan ideas about something called a *tulpa*. According to the ancient doctrines, a tulpa was a creature created by the power of thought, rather like a character in a novel, but so vividly visualized that others could actually see it.

But hearing tales about tulpas was one thing; seeing one with her own eyes was quite another. Yet the thing following her artist friend certainly seemed to fit the description. She was so fascinated she decided to find out if she could create one for herself.

The Tibetan method of tulpa creation is easy to explain, but difficult to put into practice. The technique is essentially that described in the earlier chapter about the yidam. You practice the visualization of an entity until it becomes a waking hallucination, then intensify the visualization until the "hallucination" can be seen by other people. It is advisable to begin by imagining inanimate objects, like a box or a flower, then working up to living creatures.

After her visitor left, Madame David-Neel began her own daily regime of visualization. She pictured a plump little monk, modeled after Friar Tuck in the Robin Hood legends.

At first she concentrated on seeing the monk in her mind's eye as vividly as possible, working hard to fill in even the smallest detail of his appearance. At this point the creature was a purely subjective construction, nothing more than a picture in her mind, a disciplined daydream. But once she could see the monk clearly in her mind's eye, she switched to visualizing him as if he were standing before her. (What changes at this point is the focus of your attention. The initial inward visualization can be carried out with your eyes shut.

Externalizing the vision only works with your eyes open. You pick your spot and pretend, by an act of will, that the visualized object exists there.)

It took some weeks, but Alexandra David-Neel eventually went beyond pretending. She began to see him as if he were physically present. The mental mechanism involved is that which produces hallucinations in cases of high fever or mental illness, except that it is now being evoked consciously as part of a deliberate process.

But while Madame David-Neel was perfectly aware she had created an hallucination, as time went by, the real weirdness began. One day she caught sight of her monk in the camp even though she had not made any effort to visualize him. He simply appeared, as if on his own accord. Two days later, he was back again, still without her input.

It may have been that she should have thought a little more about the feverish nervousness of her artist friend, for after this she saw the monk more and more often and without any attempt to visualize him at all. It was as if her exercise in Tibetan occultism was edging her toward madness.

And worse was to come. The monk underwent peculiar changes, losing weight and taking on a sinister, shifty aspect. Then came the day when one of Madame David-Neel's porters asked her about the "strange man in the brown robe" who was sneaking about the camp. The tulpa had become visible to others and had clearly moved beyond her conscious control.

The implications of Madame Alexandra David-Neel's experience are far-reaching. What happened is clear enough. Something consciously created as a fictional character eventually took on a life of its own, then escaped from her head to become part of objective reality. But how far did the process go?

The first two steps are, as noted earlier, familiar. Every novelist creates fictional characters and turns them loose in an imagined environment where (if he or she is lucky) they sometimes take on a life of their own. Nor is "life of their own" a metaphor for the creative process. What the author experiences is the characters going their own way, expressing their own thoughts, taking their own actions, and essentially developing their own story. If the author tries to intervene by imposing external disciplines, the characters will often resist. Should the author insist on making the characters conform with the author's own vision of the plot, the result is often a dull, flat novel, with characters who have mysteriously become zombies.

The process can sometimes go further. Some years ago, an off-shoot group within the Toronto Society for Psychical Research purposely created an entirely fictional character named Philip, who eventually began to communicate under séance-room conditions. In an experiment of my own, a British group created a fictional Saxon wise-woman, who subsequently possessed one of the members and held a conversation with the others.

The distinguished American science-fiction writer Ray Bradbury was so intrigued by the process that he wrote a book in which famous fictional characters of literature turned up as physical presences on Mars. But outside of this entertaining yarn, there have been few Western reports of mental creations escaping into the real world.[46]

All the same, if Tibetan teachings are correct—and they are vividly borne out by Madame David-Neel's experience—such creations really *can* cross from one reality to another, and this strongly suggests that neither mind nor matter are what we consider them to be in the West.

The entire question of mental constructions, their essential nature and their ability to influence what we still like to call objective reality, is one that deserves far more serious attention than it has yet received in the West. (*The Magical Use of Thought Forms*, a book by Dolores

---

46. Few, but still some. The British occultist Dion Fortune reported the appearance of an "astral wolf"—a visible creature with a degree of solidity and weight—that she believed was a projection of her own subconscious.

Ashcroft-Nowicki and me, is hopefully a step in the right direction, but a great deal more research is needed.)

Meanwhile, the dangers of tulpa creation are underlined not only by the apparent illness of the Lhasa artist, but by the difficulties experienced by Madame David-Neel, who decided that she had to reabsorb her monkish creation and expended several months of concentrated effort before she eventually succeeded.

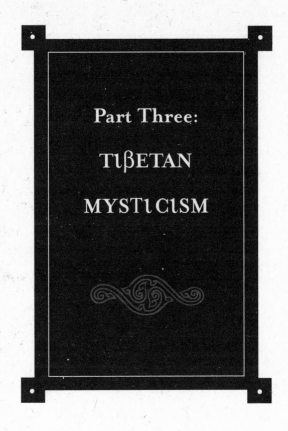

Part Three:

TIβETAN

MYSTICISM

CHAPTER TEN

KARMA AND THE SIX REALMS

Almost the whole of Tibetan mysticism is postulated on three inter-locking doctrines: the theories of rebirth, karma, and the Six Realms. The first two of these theories are familiar enough in the West—although often severely misunderstood—but the third is virtually unknown. To understand any of them correctly requires some insight into the Tibetan view of the human mind.

According to Tibetan belief, the mind is neither a physical thing, however subtle, nor, as Western psychology tends to postulate, a by-product of physical processes.[47] Rather, it is a completely formless continuum that is an entity in itself, but quite separate and distinct from body and brain.

The continuum is literally boundless—it has neither a beginning nor an end. Throughout your life, every action you take, every thought you have, impacts your subtle mind, leaving a sort of imprint. Each imprint becomes a cause that eventually generates its own particular effect. Collectively, these imprints form the engine that drives

---

47. Within the Western scientific community, it is almost commonplace to assume that what we think of as "mind" is no more than our experience of neurons firing within the brain.

karma. Thus, karma is not a judgment, not an imposition, not even an external law, but simply the inevitable result of your own thoughts and actions.[48]

One way of looking at the process is to imagine your deep mind as a field, with every action you take sowing seeds in that field. Tibetans believe that if the actions you take are virtuous, this sows the seeds of future happiness, but if you elect to behave badly, then you are sowing seeds of suffering.

Neither effect is immediate.[49] Any seed we sow remains dormant until conditions arise that permit it to germinate. For the Tibetan, that may mean a wait of several lifetimes.

According to the doctrines of Tibetan mysticism, the mind does not cease when the body dies. Our familiar experience of consciousness is lost, but only because it dissolves into the wider consciousness of the deep mind. The final section of this book will deal in detail with Tibetan ideas on the process of death, but for now, it's enough to note the belief that for most of us, our postmortem fate is to reincarnate in another body.

Although not a tenet of the major Western religions, the doctrine of reincarnation is supported by a great many well-investigated case studies like that of Imad Elawar. Elawar was born in Lebanon, in a remote, primitive village—the sort of place where time stands still and no one travels very far from home. One day he started to claim he had lived before as someone named Ibrahim Bouhamzy in a village called Khriby about thirty kilometers away. Although he repeated the claim over and over, his family did not take him seriously—until Imad bumped into somebody he recognized from his past life, a man who actually came from Khriby. The family questioned the man and discovered that he once had a neighbor—now dead—named Ibrahim Bouhamzy. This gave them the incentive to investigate, and they dis-

---

48. Karma plays itself out in the external world, of course. In a subsequent chapter on the void mind meditation technique we shall be examining how this is possible.

49. Which explains why many evil people live in comfort.

covered that forty-four of forty-seven items of information given by Imad about the Bouhamzy family were completely accurate—including the fact Ibrahim had had an affair with a woman called Jamile.

How did Imad, in a little isolated Lebanese village, know so much about what was going on in a family thirty kilometers away? The normal information sources, like newspapers or tavern gossip, can be confidently ruled out. When Imad Elawar started talking about the Bouhamzys and his mistress Jamile, he was only two years old.

There have been similar cases of spontaneous past-life recall from all over the world. Shanti Devi, Bishin Chand, and Reena Gupta, all in India, Joey Verwey in South Africa, Romy Crees in the United States, and many more are all youngsters who started to recall past lives and gave hard, detailed information that was later checked out and shown to be factually accurate.

Every instance of reincarnation, Tibetans believe, is determined absolutely by the state of your deep mind at the time of your death. If you die with a peaceful mind, this provides the conditions necessary to stimulate one of the virtuous seeds you have sown during your lifetime, and this guarantees a fortunate rebirth. But if you are foolish enough to approach death with a mind full of hatred and anger, then one of the wicked seeds you sowed begins to germinate, leading to an unfortunate rebirth.[50]

Many Westerners who accept the doctrine of reincarnation tend to assume that rebirth occurs in our familiar world at some future date. Tibetans believe differently. They accept that when sufficient karmic seeds have matured—a process which, as we shall see presently, continues for some time immediately after physical death—you will be impelled into one of six distinct realms in order to be reborn.

The Six Realms are not states of mind, but actual places.[51] During a meditation retreat in Scotland, the Venerable Geshe Kelsang Gyatso

---

50. The process is almost exactly analogous to the nightmares that arise if you retire to bed in an agitated state.

51. At least not according to the more conservative Buddhist doctrines. Some scholars argue that they are symbolic descriptions of different lifestyles.

created an interesting analogy to explain them. He invited his listeners to form a mental image of a large house. This house represents *samsara,* a philosophical term, borrowed from India, denoting the entire cycle of birth, death, and rebirth that binds life in the material world.

The house itself comprises six storys, three above ground, three below. Those sentient beings who have not yet achieved enlightenment are the inhabitants of the house, wandering from room to room (life to life) *and from story to story,* sometimes living above ground, sometimes below.

The ground floor of this imaginary house equates to the human realm, the world as you and I experience it, with all its variety, joys, and sorrows.

Immediately above the ground floor, on the first floor, lies the realm of the demi-gods. These are sentient, but nonhuman, beings who are far more powerful and prosperous than we are, but not actually all that much happier. Their fundamental problem is that they are jealous of the beings on the floor above them (the gods) and are more or less continuously at war with them. The demi-gods' obsession with jealousy and violence means that for all their power and wealth, they live impoverished lives in terms of spirituality.

On the top floor of the house is the complex realm of the gods. This floor is divided into three living quarters. The first of these, nearest the stairway that leads down to the realm of the demi-gods, is inhabited by the lowest class of real gods, the desire realm deities.

Life in the desire realm is easy and luxurious, and the deities here devote themselves to enjoyment and the fulfillment of their personal whims and ambitions. Unfortunately, this hedonistic lifestyle presents them with so many distractions that they have little motivation to engage in pursuits that would further their spiritual evolution. (Tibetan Buddhists would say they do not practice the dharma.) Paradoxically, this suggests that some inhabitants of the god realm actually have less spiritually meaningful lives than humans. Although the lifespan of the desire realm gods is very long indeed when measured against that of humans, they are not actually immortal and have a tendency to be reborn eventually in lower storys of the house.

The second of the three living quarters is the form realm. Dwellers in this realm inhabit bodies made from light. With such bodies they no longer experience sensual desire and spend their lives in a blissful state of meditation. But blissful or not, meditation is not the same thing as enlightenment, and these being too will eventually find themselves in the lower storys.

The third set of living quarters on the top floor of our imaginary house is known as the formless realm, inhabited by deities who have managed to transcend even the subtle light bodies of their neighbors and consequently experience a pervasive field of subtle consciousness similar in many respects to infinite space.

The gods of the formless realm are blessed with the purest, most exalted minds in the entire house, but even they have not managed to overcome the ignorance that creates samsara, so that over eons of time they eventually die and find themselves reborn on a lower floor.

This is a surprisingly pessimistic picture of deities, but one that makes complete sense to Tibetans, who believe that all these exalted beings are essentially caught in a very subtle trap of their own making. A succession of virtuous lives led to their birth as divinities, but life on the top floor is so seductive that they merely consume the merit they have stored up in the past while making little or no spiritual progress.

All three storys above ground—including our human world—are collectively known as the *fortunate realms* since birth in any one of them is the result of virtuous past actions and the experience of them is at least relatively pleasant. Unfortunately, the same cannot be said for the three remaining storys that have been dug below ground like basements.

Rebirth in any one of the three lower storys comes about as the result of negative (that is, nonvirtuous or immoral) thoughts, words, and actions. These gloomy basements are collectively known as the *unfortunate realms,* and life in each is miserable and frequently painful.

The least difficult of the unfortunate realms—the animal realm—lies immediately below our human world and is populated by all mammals other than ourselves, all birds, fish, insects, reptiles, and other physically living creatures. The minds of these beings are characterized by extreme stupidity. They lack spiritual awareness and their lives are governed by fear and brutality.

(This description of the animal realm—which holds to the classic Buddhist doctrines on the subject—immediately casts doubt on the concept of the Six Realms as actual separate and distinct places. Clearly, humanity and the animal kingdom both share the same world and interact continually with one another. Furthermore, the idea that all animals are brutish and stupid is belied by, among others, the elephant, chimpanzee, and dolphin. There is also a case to be made that the latter mammal may be spiritually evolved, perhaps even more highly evolved than the average human.

All of this suggests the ancient Buddhist teachings on the animal realm may now be ripe for revision. But since the present book is an exposition of Tibetan magic and mysticism rather than a critique, I shall continue to present the doctrines as taught.)

Below the animal realm, in the middle subterranean story, is the realm of the hungry ghosts. Rebirth in this realm is almost entirely caused by greed and the sort of actions driven by a miserly, ungenerous nature. The realm is one of extreme poverty, a desert world inhabited by beings who suffer continuous hunger and thirst. On the rare occasions when they manage to find so much as a scrap of food, it will typically disappear like a mirage or, worse, transform itself into a repulsive form like excrement. All experience in the realm of hungry ghosts is driven by negative karma engendered by past lives lacking in virtuous thoughts or actions.

Unpleasant though the realm of hungry ghosts may be, it is not the worst of them. Below it lies the hell realm.

Like the realm of the gods, the hell realm is divided into several living quarters. Some are fiery realms similar to medieval Christian ideas of hell. Some are vast, icy wastelands, desolate and cold. Some are realms of fearsome monsters. But all are characterized by extreme, unrelenting suffering.

Unlike Western hells, however, the torment is not eternal (although it may well feel like that). Eventually the negative karma of the hell realm inhabitants is exhausted and they are reborn elsewhere in the house of samsara with the opportunity to generate fresh karma and, perhaps, the opportunity of a more fortunate rebirth.

In presenting this comprehensive analogy, Geshe Kelsang Gyatso made the intriguing remark that the entire house was built by its inhabitants—a point we shall return to later. But once the house is in place, we and all its other inhabitants wander through the rooms like prisoners in a massive jail, sometimes enjoying the pleasures of the upper storys, but far more often suffering in the basement hells.

Is there a way out of the prison? Tibetan mysticism, like Buddhism, claims to have found an exit door.

CHAPTER ELEVEN

THE SEARCH FOR ENLIGHTENMENT

As we've already seen, the basic realization of Guatama Buddha was that the fundamental characteristic of life—all life, everywhere—is suffering. No matter how fortunate your circumstances, no matter how powerful your position, no matter how much money you have in the bank, you remain vulnerable to illness, to fear, to emotional distress, and, ultimately, to death, which strips away all your power and wealth in a single instant.

But when Guatama sat beneath his *bo*-tree, he came to realize something else: The root cause of all suffering was, and is, desire.

The popular children's writer Roald Dahl once remarked to his literary agent that while he had enough money to live in comfort for the rest of his life, he still wanted more. He was not the only one to have noticed that desire is a sliding scale. A U.K. businessman observed in a recent magazine article that had he foreseen his present situation ten years ago, he would have been convinced life could get no better. But now that the position was actually achieved, he found himself longing for a bigger car, a different house, and an even more glamorous lifestyle.

Most of us are all too familiar with this process. We begin with the heartfelt belief that all our troubles would be over if we only had ten thousand dollars stashed away. But no sooner has the target sum accumulated than we realize it's actually twenty thousand dollars we need . . . then thirty thousand . . . then forty thousand. And however much we earn, the financial requirement for security and peace of mind keeps receding like a mirage. When I was growing up, the American oil magnate J. Paul Getty was reputed to be one of the unhappiest men in the world. He was also the richest.

As the U.K. businessman discovered, the sliding scale of desire extends far beyond money or material possessions. Now that he had the wife of his (former) dreams, a nagging voice kept telling him this meant he could never sleep with his favorite movie star. Now that he had success, he thought life might be better if he had fame as well.

The elusive nature of personal satisfaction combines with another potent, if destructive, human emotion—fear of loss. It's a well-established principle in the field of marketing that fear of loss is a far stronger motivation than hope of gain. (Which is why you so often receive junk mail announcing you may have *already* won a huge prize and urging you to take action lest your chance slip away.)

Fear of loss naturally increases as old desires are fulfilled. When you lived on welfare in a trailer park, you hardly worried about burglars at all (even though your neighbors included some very suspicious-looking characters). Frankly, you had nothing worth taking. But now that you have the antique-filled mansion in Beverly Hills, you can't get enough alarm systems and guard dogs. What should have been an idyllic existence is filled with fear—for your precious property and, quite possibly, your life.

The remarkable depths of his meditation enabled Guatama to see that desire as the root of suffering pervaded every aspect of life and not just material possessions. Fall in love tomorrow and the joy comes burdened by the fear that your loved one may fall ill and die, or may not love you in return. Your greatest delight, be it your children, your career, your standing in the community, or your accumulated wealth, turns all too easily into your greatest worry.

Guatama realized that desire lay hidden at the heart of *all* suffering, even suffering where desire seems conspicuously absent. No one desires cancer or a viral infection, yet the extreme suffering that comes with these conditions arises from a desire to avoid pain or discomfort, a desire to return to a fully functioning lifestyle, a desire to avoid death, even though you know death is ultimately unavoidable. [52]

Profound though these insights might be, Buddhism would never have emerged as a world religion if Guatama had stopped there. Even if desire really is the fundamental cause of human suffering, what are you going to do about it? The pursuit of happiness isn't simply written into the American Constitution, it seems to be hard-wired into the human constitution as well. We have evolved to seek pleasure and avoid pain—both expressions of desire—so must not suffering be inevitable?

The Buddha's answer is no. However pervasive the grip of desire on the human soul, it can still be broken. And the way to break it was to cultivate *nonattachment*.

This is an idea that runs contrary to all human instinct—and even to some widespread assumptions about human morality. It's fairly easy to see the futility of attachment to possessions, even in the consumer cultures of the West, but most of us would consider loving attachment to our children to be a worthy, even noble, sentiment. Nonetheless, in the view of Buddhism, attachment remains the evil twin of desire and a consequent source of suffering.

Unfortunately the cultivation of nonattachment is far from easy. A Western reporter asked the Dalai Lama if it was true that Tibetan monks sought to detach from the world to a degree where it would make no difference to them whether they drank urine or alcohol. The Dalai Lama replied that this was the case. The reporter then asked how many Tibetan monks alive today had achieved this degree of detachment. The Dalai Lama considered the question for a moment, smiled, and told him, "I would say . . . precisely none."

---

52. If you're tempted toward the idea that pain itself is suffering (rather than the desire to avoid pain), it's worth remembering that masochists welcome it.

Whatever about the Dalai Lama's followers, many in the West would scarcely know where to begin in detaching from possessions or the things they like. Yet detachment at this level is only the start. Buddhism teaches a need for detachment from old habits of behavior and thought as well. In fact, detachment requires a whole new way of looking at the world. The question is how to achieve it.

And the answer, for most Tibetans, is meditation.

CHAPTER TWELVE

PREPARING TO MEDITATE

According to the spiritual mentor the Venerable Geshe Kelsang Gyatso, meditation is a method of acquainting your mind with virtue. Like most of his fellow Tibetans, Geshe Kelsang Gyatso believes that the more familiar your mind is with virtue, the calmer and more peaceful it becomes. Thus, meditation is not only an essential practice of what Tibetans call the *lamrim,* or path to enlightenment, but is also just about the only way of achieving anything remotely resembling a permanent state of happiness. The fundamental Tibetan belief is that since happiness is a state of mind, then the source of happiness must lie within the mind and not in external circumstances.

For many Tibetans, meditation is divided into five stages: preparation, contemplation, meditation proper, dedication, and consequent practice.

Preparation is based on three principles:

1. Purification.
2. Accumulation of merit.
3. Pursuit of blessings.

The purification process is largely internal and related to the doctrine of karma. Negative karma builds up over a series of lives and, unless the mind is purified, will tend to obstruct the growth of enlightening realizations. The accumulation of merit—an important aspect of almost all Tibetan spiritual practice—is designed to strengthen the mind in order to support liberating ideas when they begin to eventually arise.[53] The pursuit of blessings is driven by the firm belief of many Tibetans that the activation of spiritual principles within your psyche is greatly aided by blessings received from those beings who are more advanced in the realms of holiness than you are. A blessing is no empty formality. Properly imparted, it activates your potential for virtue, sustains your spiritual realizations, and helps you toward the completion of your liberation process. In short, it has a transformative effect on the mind.

The first practical step in your meditation preparations is to pick the spot you plan to use for your practice and *clean* it.

The act of cleaning has psychological as well as physical impact: it helps clear and freshen the mind as well as the place. It is also the first step toward creating a sacred space. If you plan to follow the traditional forms of Tibetan meditation, you will soon be inviting various spiritual beings to visit your immediate environment and impart their blessings. A clean and tidy meditation place is a mark of respect.

You would be well advised to extend the concept of sacred space by creating a shrine. In the current climate of political correctness, actions such as setting up a shrine are often presented as optional, in deference to the sensitivities of the agnostics and atheists among us. But in the case of Tibetan meditation, aimed at achieving liberation from samsara, there really is no option at all. The process *is* religious—or, more correctly, spiritual—and attempting to approach it in any other light tends to court failure.

For the average Tibetan, the shrine would naturally be Buddhist, incorporating representations of the Buddha's body, teachings (dharma), and mind. But the Dalai Lama himself has repeatedly

---

53. The process of liberation is as counterintuitive to the average Tibetan as it is to most Westerners. Life teaches us to grab what we can and look after Number 1. The accumulation of merit, which is the direct result of a moral lifestyle, conditions us to accept very different priorities.

emphasized the multiplicity of valid spiritual paths, so your own shrine might just as usefully feature a representation of the Lord Jesus or whichever other figure you accept as your highest spiritual ideal.

Typically, a Tibetan shrine would feature a statue of the Buddha as its centerpiece (although a picture is a perfectly acceptable substitute). On the right of the statue you would find a sacred text, representing the Buddha's teachings. To the left would be a small *stupa*,[54] representing the Buddha's mind.

Tibetan mystics consider a shrine of this type as something more than symbolic. They are convinced that the Buddha's mind—as eternal as yours and mine—will pervade the various objects, imbuing them with a life energy of their own. Consequently, once the shrine is established, you find yourself in the actual presence of a living Buddha and should act accordingly. You may feel moved to make offerings of flowers, incense, burning candles, or fruit—anything clean, beautiful, and appropriate, in fact.[55]

The recommended meditation posture is called *vajra* in Tibet and equates with the lotus pose of Hatha Yoga in which the legs are crossed in such a way that the outside of the ankles rest on the thighs. This posture is relatively easily attained by Asiatics, who have sat cross-legged for most of their lives. Westerners without yoga training often find it excruciatingly painful or downright impossible. Fortunately, the recommended posture is not an absolute necessity. The important thing is to keep the back straight (which influences the subtle energy flows within the body), so a good chair is an acceptable substitute. Place your hands in your lap, just below the navel, with your right hand on top of your left and the tips of your thumbs touching.

The first step of your inner preparations is calming the mind. This may be achieved by adopting your chosen meditation posture and

---

54. A round, often domed construction, very common in preinvasion Tibet, erected throughout the country to serve as shrines for travelers.

55. One Tibetan source suggests offerings of chocolate, which, if the Buddha is anything like me, may well be especially welcome.

taking a few minutes to concentrate on your breath. Allow yourself to breathe normally, but mentally *follow* your breathing, all the way in . . . all the way out. As you exhale, imagine that you are breathing out all of your negative aspects and distracting thoughts in the form of black smoke. Then, on the in-breath, imagine that you are taking in the blessings of all holy beings in the form of pure white light. After a few minutes, you'll find the distractions of the day melting away as your mind becomes serene.

For a Tibetan Buddhist, the next step of any meditation preparation is what's known as *seeking refuge.* If you are familiar with the common prayers of any Buddhist country, you will be aware of a frequently-repeated phrase, "I take refuge in the Buddha, the Dharma, and the Sangha"—that is, the Buddha, his doctrines and the Buddhist community. This phrase—really a prayer of sorts—is put to practical use in the preparations for Tibetan meditation.

First, you must use your intellect and imagination to create in yourself a fear of the suffering experienced in the samsaric worlds and particularly in the lower realms. Then, when you are feeling thoroughly nervous, imagine yourself (and all sentient beings) seeking refuge as you repeat the prayer, *"I and all sentient beings, until we achieve enlightenment, go for refuge in the Buddha, the Dharma, and the Sangha."* This prayer should be repeated with conviction three, seven, or even one hundred times[56] until your fear abates.

Like so much of Tibetan mysticism, refuge is seen ultimately as a mental state, and achieving refuge is directly related to strengthening the mind. This, in turn, requires a series of commitments, twelve in all, that form the background of your meditation practice.

First, you must commit not to seek refuge in teachers who contradict the Buddha's doctrines . . . *or in samsaric gods.* The first part of this commitment is more or less self-evident to the majority of Tibetans, who, of course, accept the Buddhist faith. But the second part is particularly interesting both to Buddhists and to Westerners

---

56. Or more!

who do not necessarily share the Buddhist world view. It seems to suggest that some deities—perhaps even *all* deities—are ultimately trapped in the eternal round of birth, death, and rebirth, just like everybody else.[57] This is not to say that such deities (and even those teachers who contradict the Buddha) cannot be helpful—Buddhism is an extraordinarily inclusive faith—but it is to say that, ultimately, none of them can guarantee the final liberation.

The next commitment is likely to prove more difficult to Western practitioners than to native-born Tibetans. It is the undertaking to look on any image of Buddha as an actual Buddha.

The whole question of imagery is a troubled one within the revealed religions of the West. Jehovah instructed his Chosen People not to make "graven images" of any sort: "Thou shalt not make unto thee any graven image, or any likeness of any thing that is in heaven above, or that is in the earth beneath, or that is in the water under the earth" (Exodus 20:4). Both Jews and Christians routinely ignore this directive, relying on the Biblical verse that follows[58] for the interpretation that it relates only to the *worship* of graven images. Virtually all Christian churches feature images of Jesus, and many include representations of the Virgin Mary and various saints. Islam, however, forbids imagery of any sort within its mosques, and strict Muslims even avoid its secular use in their homes.

Buddhists view the question entirely differently. Many believe that the subtle mind of Buddha, which survived the physical death of Guatama and was liberated from the necessity of rebirth, permeates Buddha images, effectively transforming them into living beings. Others take the position that an image will turn the minds of the faithful in the direction of the Buddha, permitting the formation of a mystical linkage of minds. But whatever the philosophical viewpoint, the

---

57. In this context, it is worth noting that Buddhists do not look on the Buddha as God, or *a* god. Even in his most spiritualized form he is venerated only as an individual who has achieved liberation from samsara.

58. "Thou shalt not bow down thyself to them, nor serve them: for I the LORD thy God am a jealous God . . ." (Exodus 20:5).

commitment means that a Buddha image, of whatever quality, should be treated as the Buddha himself, with offerings and prostrations generating merit for the meditator.

The third commitment is somewhat more acceptable to followers of any religion. It is simply not to harm others. Although expressed negatively, Tibetan mystics typically turn this commitment on its head and actively seek to *benefit* others. Those new to the practice are instructed first to concentrate on reducing harmful (that is, hateful, vengeful, or envious) thoughts while generating beneficial intent toward their closest family and friends.

When your heart warms toward those nearest, you can then gradually extend the same attitude toward more and more people until, eventually, you feel benevolent toward all living beings. This, like so many of the commitments, helps lay the foundation for important realizations during meditation—specifically, an understanding of the importance of love and compassion in your life.

The next commitment relates to what Tibetans refer to as the "Three Jewels." On the face of it, this is a simple enough concept, since the Three Jewels can be viewed as metaphors for the familiar objects of refuge: the Buddha, dharma, and sangha. But like so many Tibetan ideas, this one is a shade more complex. It is clear from a study of Tibetan mystical practice that the Jewels are thought of not as abstractions but as actual embodiments of Buddha, dharma, and sangha existing on some subtle level of reality. The commitment itself is to regard all dharma texts as the actual Dharma Jewel. The reasoning is that reverence for the dharma scriptures somehow creates (or perhaps reinforces) a Dharma Jewel. Here again, Westerners come up against difficulties generated by differences between Tibetan and Western ideas about the nature of mind.

Next comes a commitment not to let yourself be influenced by those who reject the Buddha's teachings. This should not be seen as an invitation to exclusivity. The practitioner is urged not to abandon those who do not share the Buddhist faith, nor to cease loving them or showing them every consideration. I would personally suspect that the commitment in no way bars serious philosophical discussion, nor the possibility of learning from other traditions. But it does caution against being led astray by the mindless adoption of bad habits or the acceptance of bad advice.

With the sixth commitment, we have reached the halfway stage in this part of our meditation preparations. This commitment instructs that ordained Buddhist priests should be regarded as an actual Sangha Jewel. Here again we have something that is perhaps a little more subtle than it appears. The Buddhist view is a long way from the familiar Roman Catholic idea of the Church as a (sole) source of spiritual authority. The commitment tends to be expressed in terms of "anyone wearing the robes of an ordained person" and comes with the added caution that it applies even where such a person is poor and of low social standing. Discussion with Tibetan spiritual teachers suggests that what is being urged here is reverence toward anyone who is holding to a moral discipline—something seen in Tibet as both rare and precious.

The seventh commitment is straightforward. It is the agreement to seek refuge in the Three Jewels time and again, in full consciousness of their qualities and the essential differences between them. One teacher has likened the dharma to a ship capable of carrying humanity across the troubled seas of samsara, the Buddha to its navigator, and the sangha to its crew. The commitment itself clearly emphasizes the need to turn one's mind with frequency and regularity toward spiritual matters if one is to hope to achieve liberation.

Reinforcing the seventh commitment is the eighth, which agrees to offer the first portion of everything we eat and drink to the Three Jewels as a mark of their kindness. This, of course, acts as a potent and repeated reminder of the spiritual path and, in Tibetan practice, is often accompanied by a prayer. Tibetans firmly believe that *all* happiness is ultimately rooted in the kindness of the Buddha, whose compassion for all sentient beings has enabled the virtuous actions that generate the positive karma that leads to happiness. Since they also believe that the spiritual Buddha manifests in different forms, including non-Buddhist teachers, it follows that all sentient creatures benefit from the Buddha's efforts whether or not they subscribe to the Buddhist faith.

The ninth commitment—to encourage others, with compassion, to seek refuge in the Buddha, dharma, and sangha—appears on the surface to have a similar dynamic to the missionary urge exhibited by some branches of Western Christianity. In Buddhism, however, this commitment is seen as an urge to advise and help, rather than impose a particular viewpoint. Practitioners are advised to act "without arrogance or impatience."

The tenth commitment is actually a more specific restatement of the seventh: the practitioner commits to seek refuge at least three times each day and three times each night. The purpose, as always, is to prepare the mind for important realizations.

For the penultimate commitment, the practitioner agrees to perform every action against a background of complete trust in the Three Jewels. This commitment carries spiritual practice beyond formal meditation preparations and into everyday life. To the Tibetan Buddhist, the commonplace Western practice of "Church on Sunday, cheat your neighbor on Monday" is not only moral anathema, but actually impractical. Since, ultimately, only the spiritual path can bring genuine benefits, any other course of action is pointless.

The final commitment is never to forsake the Three Jewels, even at the cost of your life. Buddhist teachers stress time and again that the practice of taking refuge creates the perfect conditions for those meditation realizations that lead to spiritual growth. For that reason, no price is too high to pay. Belief in reincarnation is a useful support here. Like Muslims, who believe that religious martyrs go directly to paradise, many Buddhists are convinced that those who accept death rather than abandon their refuge are reborn in the god realm.

CHAPTER THIRTEEN

PREPARATORY PREYERS

With your commitments in place, you can go on to the next substantial preparation for your meditation practice, which involves a series of short prayers uttered against the background of very specific mental states. The first of these is a prayer related to your motivation and takes the form:

> *Through such virtue as I may gain through giving and other correct actions, may I become a Buddha for the benefit of all sentient beings.*

It scarcely needs stressing here that while Westerners tend to think in terms of a single Buddha (Guatama), Tibetans accept the possibility that all sentient beings—even, surprisingly, you and me—have the potential to become Buddhas. And as followers of the Mahayana Way, it is accepted that the best possible motivation for becoming a Buddha is to help others along the same path. Human nature being what it is, this motivation may not come naturally to you, so the preparatory practice is designed to generate it through conscious effort.

The next preparation is also aimed at consciously generating a specific mental state—or, more accurately, four special states, sometimes referred to as the "four immeasurables" and encompassing love, compassion, joy, and equanimity.

Immeasurable love is generated by the wish for all sentient beings to be happy. Immeasurable compassion arises from the wish for all sentient beings to be freed from suffering. Immeasurable joy stems from the wish that all sentient beings achieve liberation from the wheel of samsara. Immeasurable equanimity appears when you wish all sentient beings freed from attachments and negative emotions like anger, hatred, or envy. Needless to say, these wishes must be genuinely felt, not simply expressed as an empty ritual, but Tibetans are convinced that such wishes need not always arise spontaneously, but can actually be generated by conscious mental and emotional effort. The prayer attached to this preparation takes the form:

> *May all sentient beings attain happiness now. May all be free from misery. May none be separated from their happiness. May all be free from hatred and attachment, thus achieving equanimity.*

The next preparation involves visualization with the accompanying "prayer" working as a verbal anchor to what is going on inside your head. The visualization itself, described in translation as "the Field for Accumulating Merit," is extremely complex in its fully developed form so that new meditation practitioners are advised to establish it stage by stage.

The first and by far the most important stage is to visualize the Buddha seated centrally in an expanded space before you. You should realize that he is surrounded by a whole host of bodhisattvas[59] and holy beings amicable to your own efforts to achieve liberation. Gradually, in the course of your meditation practice, you should try to visualize these beings as well—adding perhaps one or two every few

---

59. One who is able to reach the Clear Light but delays doing so through compassion for suffering beings.

sessions—until you can see them with your inner eye surrounding the Buddha "like stars around the full moon." This visualization is believed to develop conditions that permit your mind to accumulate merit and is accompanied by the spoken words:

> *Before me is the Living Buddha, surrounded by all Buddhas*
> *and bodhisattvas, like the full moon surrounded by stars.*

Following on the visualization of the Field for Accumulating Merit is a practice known as the Prayer of Seven Limbs, which does indeed involve a prayer, but is primarily a series of actions designed to purify negativity and generate merit.

The first of the seven limbs is prostration, something that comes more easily to Tibetans than to the proud individualists of the West. Nonetheless, a full, physical prostration is a sign of respect—in this instance toward the holy beings visualized in the Field for Accumulating Merit—as are verses of praise and the mental attitude of faith. All three forms of respect are recommended in this part of the exercise, but if you are too old and stiff, or otherwise unwell, to accomplish a full physical prostration, an acceptable substitute is to place your hands together, palms touching, at the level of your heart. But before you feel tempted to adopt this substitute without good reason, it's as well to remember that full physical prostration serves to reduce your level of pride, and consequently increases your chances of achieving liberation.

The second limb is the making of offerings. The question of offerings has already been covered to some extent when we examined how to set up a meditation shrine. But Tibetan mystics, whose understanding of visualization clearly differs from that prevalent in the West, believe that offerings created in the imagination will be just as acceptable to the holy beings. The keyword here seems to be *created*. A real effort is required to create and visualize gifts worthy of offering. Allow your imagination to roam free. Remember that you are no longer limited by the size of your bank balance. You may wish to offer a fine

Arab stallion, a crystal rock pool, a rare vial of exquisite perfume, or even, as one teacher suggested, an entire cosmos. But these examples are not given as templates. The holy beings gain nothing from your offerings, but by creating individual gifts of your own, you will accumulate merit and, incidentally, set a psychological process in motion that will counteract any tendency you might have toward meanness.

The third limb is confession. Roman Catholic readers will be familiar with the process, as will those who have engaged in secular therapies like psychoanalysis, but once again the thrust of the Tibetan approach is somewhat different. Here you are not seeking forgiveness—from a deity, a wronged one, or even from yourself—but rather hoping to purify your mind.

Thus, the first step in Tibetan mystical confession is to contemplate the process of karma. This will quickly lead to the realization that you have engaged in a great many actions of which you are not particularly proud. An understanding of karma will alert you to the consequences of such actions. This in turn will arouse a wish to purify the negativity generated by your actions and, by so doing, escape the painful working out of karma that is otherwise inevitable.

The purification process is straightforward. It starts with your recognition of the faults that were embedded in your actions and genuine regret for what you did. Tibetan mystics point out that regret is not the same thing as guilt (which is itself a negative emotion). Guilt is a helpless wallowing that goes nowhere itself and tends to block positive action. Regret is in its essence a wish to purify the mind of negativity—specifically, the negativity generated by the karma of our past faults.

As the wish arises, you should confess those faults to the beings you have visualized standing before you in the Field for Accumulating Merit, thus attracting their support and blessing in your efforts to purify your karma. Confession should be accompanied by an absolute determination not to repeat past mistakes.

The process of confession is a purification in itself, but perhaps even more importantly, it creates conditions in which future virtuous actions not only generate beneficial karma, but also tend to cancel out accumulated negativity.

The fourth limb is to positively rejoice in virtue. This is particularly interesting to practitioners in the West, where virtue can sometimes be looked upon as a grim business requiring rigid self-control and sober clothing. For the smiling Tibetan, virtue in ourselves and others is a cause for celebration. And such celebration goes a very long way toward overcoming envy and competitiveness, thus greatly increasing your accumulated store of merit. Interestingly, some Tibetan mystics consider that even on its own, the celebration of virtue in others can become one of your most powerful spiritual practices.

The fifth limb involves calling on the holy beings in your Field for Accumulating Merit to remain with you always. This simple, almost obvious, prayer has some subtle implications. Implicit in it, for example, is the recognition of your own spiritual frailty and your need for the help and support of those who have trod the path before you. Most Tibetans accept that each of us has a specific Spirit Guide whose "job" it is to help us follow a virtuous road through this life and future lives. The Guide may be the Buddha himself, a bodhisattva, or some other highly evolved entity, perhaps even a deity. But in any case, he or she will appear among the multitude of beings in the Field for Accumulating Merit, and the call of the fifth limb underlines your determination to retain your connection with the spiritual realities in the days ahead.

The sixth limb is a formal request to receive the dharma or words of the Buddha. Such a request may appear superfluous for Tibetans who have been steeped in the dharma from birth, and possibly even for Westerners, who have devoted time to the study of Buddhist scriptures. Nonetheless, Tibetan mystics believe the sixth limb to be important since making the request is itself a karmic action that creates a cause for Buddhist doctrines to remain in our world. This clearly has a general benefit, but even from a purely selfish viewpoint[60] it ensures

---

60. Which is not, of course, encouraged.

that the guidance of the dharma will remain available to you in future lives.

The seventh and final limb is the dedication of merit. The meaning of this limb is not at all obvious until you become familiar with the Tibetan mystical viewpoint. In the West, merit is often seen by moral philosophers as an end in itself: you do the right thing precisely because it *is* right. For the average Tibetan, merit is a means to an end—usually the guarantee of a fortunate rebirth. For the Tibetan mystic, however, the only really worthwhile use of accumulated merit is the achievement of enlightenment.

Against this background, it is easy to see the importance of dedicating such merit as you may generate during your meditations not toward the samsaric end of a comfortable reincarnation, but toward the ultimate goal of achieving enlightenment for you and for all sentient beings. It is, in short, a matter of focusing and directing your *intent*.

The prayer that embodies the seven limbs is worded along the lines of:

> *Humbly I prostrate with body, speech, and mind.*
> *Offerings I make in this realm and the inner worlds.*
> *My wrong deeds I confess from lifetimes without number.*
> *Observe the joy I take in all the virtues that are manifest*
> *in the world*
> *And remain with me as my guides and mentors until samsara ends,*
> *Turning for all beings the great Wheel of Dharma.*
> *To the enlightenment of all sentient beings, I dedicate such merit as I may accumulate in my meditation practice.*

The preliminary practice that follows the prayer of the seven limbs is something so specifically Tibetan that one doubts it could have been developed in any other culture. The practice is called "offering the mandala."

Mandala, as noted earlier, is a term derived from Sanskrit where it means simply "circle." It was introduced to a wide intellectual audience in the West by the Swiss psychologist Carl G. Jung when he published studies of mandala-like drawings produced spontaneously by several of his patients. Jung theorized that the drawings represented an attempt by the conscious self to integrate unconscious material and was thus an important step in the individuation process on which his whole school of psychology was based. Whatever about this, the therapeutic effect of spontaneous mandala creation was marked, suggesting a profound link between the symbol and the basic structure of the human mind.

In Hindu and Buddhist Tantra, however, mandalas are symbolic diagrams used in sacred rites and meditation. Each mandala is fundamentally a representation of the universe and, again, as noted in an earlier chapter, serves as a sacred space in which the gods may manifest and universal forces collect. By mentally entering a mandala and working your way toward its center, you are guided through the cosmic processes of disintegration and reintegration.

To create the mandala you will use as a preliminary to meditation, you should begin by imagining that you are holding in both hands an enormous golden disc that will form the base of the mandala proper. In the center of the disc, visualize the towering form of Mount Meru.

In Tibetan[61] mythology, Meru is a golden mountain that stands in the center of the universe and acts as the axis of our world, reaching as deeply into the nether regions as it soars into the heavens above. It is the abode of the gods, and its foothills are the great Himalayas.

Your visualization should see Meru surrounded by four island continents, with the sun and moon hanging high above its peak. Beyond the continents, you may imagine the pure, beautiful aspects of the world set out in perfect balance.

---

61. And, indeed, Hindu.

Offering the Mandala as a preliminary to meditation is a formalized way of causing the entire universe, symbolically transformed into the Buddha's Pure Land, to enter your Field for Accumulating Merit.

(An important Buddhist sutra tells the story of Amitabha, a monk who, many eons ago, learned from the eighty-first Buddha about the glories of various Buddha Lands. He was so impressed that he vowed there and then to create his own Buddha Land, eighty-one times better than all the others. He promised that when this Pure Land was fashioned, it would be open to all sentient creatures who invoked his name. The sutra adds that in addition to calling on Amitabha, you need to accumulate merit and strive toward enlightenment.)

The prayer that accompanies the offering is worded as follows:

> *The ground of my world is perfumed and flower-strewn: the great Mount Meru, the four lands, the sun, and the moon, forming Buddha's Pure Land and so offered. May all beings find the joys of such Pure Lands.*

To complete the offering, you should now symbolically hand over all those things that strengthen your attachment to samsara—your obsession with material possessions, your love of money, your urge toward the work ethic, competitive thoughts, and even the people (both friends and enemies) with whom you have strong links. In Buddhist thought there are Three Poisons: attachment, hatred, and confusion. Everything that contributes to the Three Poisons should be imaginably transformed into purified beings and enjoyments, then offered to the Three Jewels, thus weakening the basis on which such delusional attachments form. This offering is accompanied by a prayer in the following form:

> *Without sense of loss, I offer all and everything that gives rise to my attachment, hatreds, and confusion—my friends, enemies, and strangers, our loves, hates, and enjoyments, body and mind. Accept them, I pray, and extend to me thy blessing*

so that I may be released from all attachment, hatred, and confusion.

The final preparation is an act of imagination and belief. When you have completed the mandala offering, extend your imagination to realize that all the Buddhas and bodhisattvas in your Field for Accumulating Merit are smiling at you in delight. Now visualize the central Buddha as beginning to radiate powerful streams of pure light and enchanted nectar from his heart chakra. Feel these streams entering through the crown of your head until your entire body is filled with their radiance and bliss.

Know with absolute certainty that what is happening is more than imagination, since your visualization has opened up a channel for spiritual energies to pour through. What you are receiving is a literal blessing from the Buddha that will purify your mind and sweep away any hindrances that might block a profound meditation experience and prevent you from achieving your most important realizations.

The preparations outlined may appear onerous at first glance, but this is largely because of the space needed to explain them to a non-Tibetan (and, quite possibly, to a non-Buddhist) reader. Once you become familiar with what's needed, the preparations themselves will be carried through quickly, easily, and efficiently. They lead quite naturally to the final blessing, which, you will discover, leaves your mind clear, positive, and powerful.

At this point you are ready to begin meditation.

CHAPTER FOURTEEN

TIBETAN MEDITATIONS

It is important to recognize that "meditation" is an umbrella term for several different mental processes. In the West, it often simply denotes any disciplined use of the mind, or prolonged examination of a specific subject. In Tibet, two broad categories of meditation are recognized: analytical and contemplative.

Analytical meditation is similar to the Western form in which the mind is first persuaded, then taught, to focus on a given train of thought, based on a chosen subject or text, usually of a spiritual nature. In the Tibetan tradition, however, the subject or text is almost always the dharma, the teachings of the Lord Buddha.

Thus, Tibetan analytical meditation begins not with meditation itself, but with listening to, or reading, Buddhist doctrines. In your subsequent meditation session, you examine those doctrines, attempting to understand exactly what they mean and to determine their relevance to your life.

Contemplative meditation often follows on analytical meditation and arises naturally from it. Here you select a specific aspect of the dharma and concentrate on it to the exclusion of all else, becoming more and more deeply acquainted with it until you reach a conclusion or cause a virtuous state of mind to arise. Essentially the same result may be obtained by selecting a spiritual object or person as the subject of your contemplation. Here again in Tibet, the chosen object almost always has a Buddhist association.

When your meditation is finished, you should visualize the various holy beings in your Field for Accumulating Merit as dissolving into pure white light, which in turn enters your body through the crown chakra at the top of your head. This visualization, vividly performed, can in itself have a profound effect on your mind, something you should encourage by imagining yourself becoming one with the Buddha. This merging with Buddha consciousness is, of course, a spiritual elevation that tends to carry you further along the path of liberation and enlightenment.

You should complete each meditation session with a prayer of dedication, offering any merit you may have accumulated to the happiness and liberation of all sentient beings. The formal expression of the prayer might be along the following lines:

> *Whatsoever merit I have stored in my meditation practice, I hereby dedicate to all living beings, that they, too, may find an opportunity to engage in their own practice of the dharma. I pray that all may experience happiness and swiftly reach enlightenment so that the trap of samsara is finally broken.*

If you have the leisure to devote your time entirely to spiritual pursuits, you can speed your progress toward eventual enlightenment by meditating four times each day, beginning in the early morning. Your second session should begin before lunch, your third in the late afternoon, and the final meditation period late in the evening to prepare your mind for sleep.

Those of you whose lives are filled with more samsaric concerns may still make considerable progress by engaging in as little as one meditation session per day, provided you practice regularly. Even a few minutes of daily meditation is far better than bursts of several hours at irregular intervals. Beginners may find that early morning is best for a single daily meditation, when the mind is fresh and as yet unburdened by the concerns of the day. Later, when you gain proficiency, you can try switching your meditation time to the evening. Tibetans believe that meditation before sleep permits the mind to achieve realizations and/or generate merit during the sleeping state. Beginners, however, often find that an evening meditation attempt will send you directly to sleep before any real meditation gets underway, thus short-circuiting the whole process.

How much time you devote to meditation practice is largely a question of personal choice and other commitments. Many Tibetan spiritual teachers would recommend a half hour period to begin with, gradually increased to a maximum of two hours if circumstances permit. It is often a good idea to meditate on the same subject matter for several consecutive days, something that will permit deeper and deeper realizations to arise.

Clearly, the Buddhist canon contains more than enough material to engage your meditations for a lifetime—or several lifetimes, as Buddhists themselves believe. For Tibetans on the mystic path, guidance in the meditation subjects they might initially select would typically be offered by their guru. Readers of the present book (who may not have found their guru yet) might usefully begin[62] with the selection of meditation subjects that follow, based on a retreat schedule created by Geshe Kelsang Gyatso and well suited to beginning meditators who are interested in the Tibetan path.

Subject 1: Your Spiritual Guide

As noted in earlier chapters, Tibetans do not believe in going it alone when it comes to spiritual matters. For most of them, a skilled spiritual guide is the absolute underpinning of all spiritual progress.

---

62. But it can't be stressed strongly enough that this is only a *beginning*. Meditation is a life's work, and you will need far more guidance than you can find in a single chapter of a single book.

In this meditation, you are advised to consider the advantages of following a qualified spiritual guide,[63] then contemplate the benefits until a determination arises to rely on the guide wholeheartedly. Hold this determination single-pointedly for as long as possible in the meditation session.

It is important to avoid negative thoughts about your guide during meditation—and, indeed, thereafter—since these tend to weaken your faith. As always in Tibetan meditation, any such thoughts that do intrude should not be suppressed, but simply ignored (Tibetans would say "let go"). Attempting to suppress a thought gives it power. Thoughts that are ignored during meditation simply fade away.

(This meditation subject remains a good starting point even if you have not yet found your spiritual guide. Analyzing the advantages of such a guide will strengthen your resolve to seek out someone who can help you.)

Subject 2: The Value of a Human Life

The subject matter here is not "The Value of Human Life," however worthy a topic that might be in these troubled times. Rather, it is "The Value of *a* Human Life"—phraseology that places it firmly within the Tibetan Buddhist context. Your initial analysis should focus on how fortunate you are to have been born a human and not, for example, an animal or hungry ghost.

From this starting point, you might usefully expand your examination to embrace your own circumstances as a human. However miserable or impoverished you may believe your life to be, you have still been presented with an opportunity to study and practice the Buddhist *dharma*.[64]

Contemplate the realizations that arise until you achieve a deep and genuine appreciation of the value your life has as a vehicle for

---

63. The term *qualified* is used here not in the sense of someone who has made an academic study of the subject, but rather one who is advanced on the spiritual path—something that may have attracted no paper qualifications whatsoever.

64. The very fact you are reading this book contributes to the realization, in however small a way.

spiritual practice, and attempt single-pointedly to hold the feeling of appreciation for as long as possible.

When you have successfully achieved the desired result, you might like to extend this meditation by a second-stage analysis of the benefits of dharma practice. (In your first analysis, you simply examined the value of a human life in terms of the opportunity it presented in relation to the dharma. Here you analyze the value of dharma practice itself.)

Contemplate the realizations that arise until you generate a determination to practice the dharma as your life's priority, without the waste of a single precious moment. Hold this determination single-pointedly for as long as possible in your meditation session.

Subject 3: Death

The concept of impermanence lies at the very heart of Buddhist doctrine and represents an idea that runs so contrary to our mundane attitudes that it requires a real effort to grasp. We tend to think of the outside world as permanent and unchanging, something that will always be there for us and, above all, the one thing that is of prime importance in our lives. We may intellectually accept the value of Buddhist precepts, but attachment to worldly activities—pursuit of power, wealth, and position, sexual attraction, desire for security, or even the simple need to earn a living—radically dilutes any real wish we may have to spend time in dharma practice.

This is a very common obstacle and one that clearly needs to be overcome if you are to achieve enlightenment, liberation, or even just a fortunate rebirth. Tibetan mystics believe that the best—perhaps the only—way to overcome the obstacle is to gain a deep emotional realization that the very goals we consider most important are actually impermanent states and thus not worth a candle. And the way to achieve this realization, difficult though it may be for a Westerner, is to meditate on death.

You might usefully begin your analysis by plunging in at the deep end with the startling realization that even you will die one day. We all know we will die, of course, but only as an intellectual exercise. Imagine the difference in your behavior if your doctor told you tomorrow that you had terminal cancer. Yet this diagnosis is no more than a confirmation of your mortality—something you have lived with all your life.

From the realization that you will die some time (and there is absolutely no way to prevent it), you can go on to examine the fact that death may not be something postponed to a distant old age. It could happen today. It could, God forbid, even happen before you finish reading this page.

Confronting death in this way generates a realization of your own impermanence and consequently the impermanence of your worldly activities. You can strengthen this realization by contemplating the absolute truth that you may die today. (Some spiritual teachers recommend repeating the words "I may die today" over and over during the course of the meditation.)

It takes a real degree of effort, but eventually you will begin to feel the *certainty* of this realization, and with that certainty will come a new mindset. Understanding that you could depart from this world at any second generates detachment from mundane pressures and enjoyments and ignites the arousal of fresh priorities—a deep and genuine concern for spiritual progress toward enlightenment and liberation.

Subject 4: Karma

The perceived conflict in Western philosophy between theories of free will and predetermination is neatly resolved in Tibetan Buddhism. According to the ancient dharma, the sort of person you are and the situation in which you find yourself *is* predetermined—but only by the exercise of your free will in the past. Actions, thoughts, and attitudes undertaken earlier in this life and throughout a long chain of previous incarnations all contribute to your burden of karma, which absolutely determines where you stand at this moment, but simultaneously presents the mechanism by which you can control what and where you will be in the future.

Your analysis of karma might begin at that point, perhaps examining the theory of reincarnation, but even more importantly, seeking to understand the accessible psychological processes by which we all create our own destinies. Try to understand how avoidance of legitimate pain—such as that involved in taking a stand against evil, for example—can lead to much greater pain later on. Seek out the relationship between cause and effect, the thoughts that lead to attitudes, the attitudes that lead to actions, and the actions that impinge back on our inner processes, generating stress, strife, and unhappiness.

You will eventually reach the point of realization that virtuous actions have a tendency, even in the short and medium terms, to lead to increased happiness and peace of mind.

Contemplation of such realizations will develop a conviction of the truth of karma and a determination to avoid nonvirtuous thoughts and actions in the future. This in itself is an important practice of the dharma, and one that will carry you a long way toward liberation.

CHAPTER FIFTEEN

MANTRA

One of the more important tools of Tibetan mysticism is the mantra, a sacred syllable, word, or verse considered to possess some degree of spiritual power. While many, perhaps even most, mantras have little apparent verbal meaning, they are widely believed to be a distillation of spiritual wisdom. But the full force of the mantra lies in what it does rather than what it is. In practical terms, mantras are either spoken aloud or sounded internally in order to achieve a specific result. A repeated mantra may be an aid to meditation, a meditation in itself, or the object of meditation. But before examining the use of the mantra in meditation, it is necessary to realize that, historically, Tibetans have viewed and used sound very differently from the cultures of the West.

There have, for example, been reports of a mysterious Tibetan technology of sound which, while it did not survive in its totality into the twentieth century, nevertheless left some fascinating traces. The prime source of these reports is a work entitled *Försvunnen teknik,* by the Swedish author Henry Kjellson, published in 1961. At time of writing,[65] I have failed to locate an English language edition of the book, but the publishers Nihil, in Copenhagen, issued a Danish

---

65. 2004.

translation in 1974 and the British author Andrew Collins drew on this for his own account.[66]

What Kjellson had to say was fascinating. He told of a Swedish doctor known simply as "Jarl" who was invited by a Tibetan friend during the 1930s to visit a monastery southwest of Lhasa. During his stay, he was taken to a nearby cliff. About 250 meters up the cliff face was a cave entrance fronted by a broad ledge. Here the monks were building a stone wall.

As you might imagine, this was no easy site to reach. The only access to the cave was ropes, which the monks had strung down from the top of the cliff. Jarl saw no sign of lifting machinery for the stones, but about the same distance from the base of the cliff as the ledge was above it, there was a large, bowl-shaped boulder embedded in the ground. Behind it was a substantial group of monks. Jarl's attention was drawn to several of them who carried large drums and long trumpets.

As Jarl watched, a monk used a knotted piece of measuring rope to position thirteen drums and six trumpets in a 90-degree arc around the bowl-stone. About ten monks formed a line behind each instrument while there were three more monks with drums at the center of the arc. The middle man had a small drum hung around his neck. The monks on either side had larger drums hung from wooden frames, while on either side of these there were monks holding three-meter long trumpets. Beyond them were even more drums slung from frames, one pair being the largest Jarl saw. Further out along the arc, drums alternated with trumpets. All the drums were open at one end, and this end was pointed toward the bowl-stone.

A sled drawn by a yak dragged a large stone block to the bowl-stone, where it was manhandled into the depression by a group of monks. The monk at the center of the arc then began to chant and beat the small drum. The rhythm was taken up by the trumpets, then the larger drums, gradually increasing in pace until the sound seemed continuous.

---

66. In *Gods of Eden*, by Andrew Collins (London: Headline, 1998).

This went on for three or four minutes. Then the block in the center of the bowl-stone wobbled. As it did so, the monks slowly tilted their instruments—both trumpets and drums—upward. The block rose with them as if levitated by the sound, and followed an arced trajectory toward the cave-mouth high above. When it reached the ledge, the sound stopped and it crashed down, ready for use in the wall. Another block was then dragged to the bowl-stone.

Kjellson reported further evidence of Tibetan levitation by sound in the experience of an Austrian moviemaker he called "Linauer," who also visited a remote Tibetan monastery in the 1930s. There he was shown an enormous gong made up of a golden center section ringed with hoops of iron and brass. He was also shown a bowl-shaped stringed instrument (rather like an open lute) two meters long and a meter wide, which, like the gong, was cast using three different metals. The thing was so large it had to be supported by a wooden frame.

The gong and the bowl were used together with two large screens set to form a triangle. When the gong was struck, it set up sympathetic vibrations in the strings of the bowl. The screens directed the sound toward a large stone block. After striking the gong repeatedly, a monk was able to lift the block with one hand, even though it appeared far too heavy. The monk claimed that "long ago" instruments of this type had been used to build defensive walls "round the whole of Tibet." He also said that similar devices emitted sounds that would shatter stone and dissolve matter. This seems a ridiculous claim, yet the British biologist and author Dr. Lyall Watson reports[67] on an incident in France that demonstrates exactly the same phenomenon in modern times.

According to Watson, an engineering professor named Gavraud was subject to recurring bouts of nausea while at work in his Institute in Marseilles. The sickness became so bad that he was at the point of giving up his job. The only thing that stopped him was the suspicion that it was something in his environment that was causing the trouble. He began to run tests.

---

67. In *Supernature* (London: Hodder & Staughton, 1973).

His first thought was chemical pollutants. At the time (early 1970s) there had been problems with the constituents of certain building materials and some fabric cleaners. But tests for the more likely culprits proved negative. Professor Gavraud then tested for more obscure chemicals and even radioactivity, still with negative results. He was at the point of giving up when chance intervened. Leaning against a wall of his office—which was on the top floor of the building—he became aware of a slight vibration. Soon he realized that the whole room was filled with a very low frequency subsonic hum.

Gavraud set about tracing the hum to its source, and discovered that the root cause was an air conditioning plant on the roof of the building opposite. By sheer coincidence, it happened that his office was exactly the right shape and distance away to resonate with the machinery. The basic rhythm—seven cycles a second—was what was making him ill.

The discovery fascinated Gavraud. He decided to build something that could generate infrasound so he could investigate it further. He cast about for a likely prototype and found that the standard issue police whistle carried by all gendarmes actually generated a whole range of low frequency sounds. Using this as a model, he built a police whistle six feet long, powered by compressed air.

When the device was tested—by a technician rather than Gavraud himself—Tibetan theories about the destructive power of sound were dramatically vindicated. On the first blast, the technician collapsed. Medical examination showed he had died instantly. A post-mortem reported that his internal organs had been turned to jelly.

Despite the tragedy, Gavraud pressed on with his experiments, but with precautions. His next test was conducted out of doors and the observers were sheltered in a concrete bunker. The compressed air was turned on very gradually, but even so the sound broke every window within half a mile of the test site.

Before long, Gavraud learned how to control the amplitude of the sound vibrations and also how to build much smaller infrasound generators. He also discovered that the sound could be specifically focused. By directing two sound beams at a target building, the structure could be demolished at distances up to five miles.

While the Gavraud experiments are strong confirmation of Tibetan claims about the destructive power of sound, it is less easy to take seriously the idea that sound can also be used to affect the weight of solid objects and even levitate massive stone blocks. All the same, there seems to be some confirmation of these claims as well.

Although the American inventor John Ernst Worrell Keely—who lived and worked during the Late Victorian era—has long been described as a fraud, recent scholarly investigations have failed to find any motive for fraud and suggest that some of his inventions may actually have been viable.

The importance of this is that if Keely really *was* genuine, several of his devices support the Tibetan reports that sound might be used to influence the weight of, or even levitate, solid objects. Keely had an obsession with overcoming gravity. In 1881, he claimed he had invented a secret device to lift heavy weights for a client in California. Like many other engineers of his day, he was interested in the creation of flying machines, but he never envisaged the powered flight with which we are familiar today. Nor did he see the problem in terms of gliding or the wing movements of birds. His approach was a principle he dubbed "vibrational lift," which seems to have involved some sort of sound-generated levitation.

Keely demonstrated vibrational lift again and again. In the spring of 1890, he used it to raise a model airship weighing eight pounds, but claimed, "An airship of any number of tons of weight can, when my system is completed, float off into space with a motion as light as thistledown . . . " The American writer and theosophist R. Harte described how Keely "introduced a certain force" to an iron cylinder weighing several hundredweights, after which he was able to lift it with one finger. Keely's patron, Mrs. Bloomfield-Moore, claimed he was able to carry a five-hundred horsepower engine from one part of his workshop to another with the aid of levitational appliances. A Philadelphia newspaper carried a story attested by an eyewitness named Jefferson

Thomas that Keely had levitated a six-thousand pound metal sphere—possibly the one discovered under his workshop after his death.

In a more controlled experiment, Keely caused grocer's weights to float in water when he plucked on the strings of a harplike instrument. In 1893, Jacob Bunn, a vice president of the Illinois Watch Company, saw Keely set heavy steel balls moving through the air "simply by playing on a peculiar mouth organ." The Boston scientist Alfred H. Plum witnessed Keely drive machinery and cause a two-pound metal sphere to float and sink in water by sounding different notes on a trumpet.

All this sounds like support for the stories of sonic levitation that have emerged from Tibet, but Keely's reputation remains a problem. Despite an apparent lack of motivation and the other factors mentioned, his actions were undoubtedly suspicious. For a man who claimed to have invented an almost endless stream of incredible devices, he took out precious few patents—an ongoing bone of contention between his shareholders and himself.

Fortunately, the testimony of nineteenth-century witnesses—who *may* have been fooled by the equivalent of clever conjuring—is not the only thing we have to go on when evaluating claims of a sonic technology in ancient Tibet. As I reported in another of my books,[68] the art of sonic levitation seems to be alive and well in Tibet's next door neighbor, India—or at least was alive and well within living memory.

In 1961, Englishwoman Patricia (Paddy) Slade, now widowed and living near Bath, visited India with her British Army husband Peter. During a stay in Poona, they were advised by a friend to see a particularly interesting religious ceremony scheduled to take place in the city.

The ceremony, which was held in the open air, involved a total of eleven white-robed priests and a boulder, which Paddy Slade estimated to weigh around forty tons. The priests circled the stone while

---

68. *A Secret History of Ancient Egypt* (London: Piatkus, 2000).

chanting. On the eleventh circuit, the chanting stopped, each priest placed a fingertip on the rock, and together they lifted it shoulder high. They held it in the air for a little under half a minute, then set it down again.

To show no trickery was involved, the priests asked for volunteers to repeat the performance. Paddy Slade was among those who stepped forward. With others from among the spectators she circled the stone, chanting. Then came the attempt to lift it. To her astonishment it rose as easily as it had done for the priests.

If, as now seems likely, we have to take seriously the Tibetan claims of a sonic technology, it is interesting to note that it seems to have survived, at least in some of its aspects, up to the present day. Madame Alexandra David-Neel reports[69] on a meeting with a "master of sound" in a Bön monastery at Tesmon.

Preparations were being made for a ceremony when a disruption occurred. A man who had entered was ordered to leave by the monks and became extremely abusive. The Bön Lama picked up a type of ritual bell, called a *chang,* and used it to produce waves of disharmonious vibrations. The intruder screamed, fell backward, and left hurriedly.

Madame David-Neel followed the man, who claimed that a "snake of fire" had come out of the chang. Others who had witnessed the event said that they had seen no snake, but that flashes of light had come out of the instrument. Madame David-Neel herself had seen nothing.

Later, when she asked the Bön Lama about the incident, he told her that what the witnesses had seen was the power of the spell[70] he had cast with the aid of the chang. He suggested that the sound somehow created shapes and even beings. Interestingly, when he rang the bell again for Madame David-Neel, it no was longer discordant, but produced a "melodious carillon" of sound.

---

69. In *Bandits, Priests and Demons* (The Hague, Holland: Uitgeverij Sirius en Siderius, 1988).

70. The word used was *gzungs,* which denotes a magical formula and carries the sense of something that grips.

Both Bön and Buddhist monasteries make considerable use of sound as part of their spiritual practice. Virtually every surviving temple has its own "orchestra," but the work of that orchestra seems to be something other than the production of music as it is known in the West. Its function is to create specific combinations of sounds as an aid to activities like meditation. Furthermore, there is an intriguing linkage with the human body. In 1983, a theatrical piece was presented in Holland, based on the electronic amplification of various body sounds like heartbeat and blood flow within the veins. Among those who attended the performance was the writer and traveler Erik Bruijn, who had spent considerable time studying Tibetan temple practice. He noted at once the striking similarities between the sounds he was hearing and those he had heard in Tibet. By the time the performance was finished, he had concluded that the typical Tibetan temple orchestra was set up to reproduce precisely the sounds generated naturally within the human body.

The most common use of sound in meditation is the mantra, used as a tool to "throw off" extraneous thoughts. Even a simple mantra, such as the syllable *om*, can be effective in concentrating the mind when repeated internally or aloud, and may lead to trance states in a susceptible subject. An even more effective technique involves the use of a circular mantra, such as the expanded *om mani padme hum*, developed in India and imported into Tibet as a significant part of Buddhist practice.

Om mani padme hum[71] should be sounded sonorously and continuously, with the final humming *m* blending seamlessly into the initial *om*—phonetically in Tibetan: *aum manee peh-meh hunggaum manee pe-meh hunggaum manee peh-meh hung,* and so on. If you practice this aloud until it becomes a rising and falling sine wave of humming sound, you will quickly discover that it acts as a meditation focus, neatly fixing the mind on the subject at hand. After a time, as

---

71. Which is sometimes translated as "Hail to the Jewel in the Lotus," although the actual meaning seems to be irrelevant to its mantric use.

the practice grows familiar, you will be able to replicate the sound mentally, where it will have essentially the same effect.

Virtually any circular mantra produces this result to a greater or lesser degree—you've probably already noticed how difficult it is to get a catchy chorus from a pop song out of your head—but Tibetan use of mantras is a far more complex and subtle matter than this.

To begin with, the mantric sound *om* is believed in Tibet, as in India, to be the fundamental vibration of the universe,[72] while other sounds used in mantras are thought to have specific physical effects. Indeed, Tibetan mystics are convinced there is an absolute interplay of body, speech, and mind in any effective religious practice.

The body plays its part through postures, prostrations, offerings,[73] and *mudras* (specific gestures of the hands and fingers believed to influence the body's energy channels).

The mind is involved through its visualizations of the holy beings, as noted in the previous chapter, and through the creation of mental equivalents of the physical offerings. All techniques of Tibetan mysticism are based on the conviction that only your mind can evoke the forces to which your visualizations of the holy beings—and, indeed, your offerings—correspond. Without mental involvement, religious ceremonial becomes an empty sham.

Speech contributes by way of prayer and the mantric use of sound. (In certain instances, the two are one and the same.) Tibetan mystics maintain that certain mantras help call into being their various mental creations and bring about a transformation from mere images to living beings. Other mantras are useful in converting material offerings into subtle equivalents, more suited to their divine recipients. Still others help focus the mind on difficult concepts. And, as we have seen, some function to clear the mind prior to and during meditation.

The principle that underlies much of Tibetan mantra usage is quite alien to Western scientific thought, but more familiar in Western

---

72. Whatever about this, it would certainly appear that our planet has a fundamental vibration, a resonance discovered by scientists only in the late twentieth century.

73. There is a tactile aspect to offerings since the individual items are necessarily touched.

religious practice and accessible to personal experience. For example, clear indications of a belief in the creative use of sound appear the Christian Gospels: "In the beginning was the Word and the Word was with God and the Word was God" (John 1:1), and again, "And the Word was made flesh, and dwelt among us (and we beheld his glory, the glory as of the only begotten of the Father), full of grace and truth" (John 1:14).

The word *amen* uttered sonorously at the end of a prayer may have mantric significance. Although conventionally derived from Hebrew via New Testament Greek and translated as "So be it," a minority school of thought traces the root to Ancient Egypt, where the deity Amen (also transliterated as "Amun," "Amon," or "Ammon") was revered as King of the Gods. If this latter derivation is correct, then the Christian, Jewish, and Muslim use of *amen* may be closer to a Tibetan mantra than the faithful realize.

Experiential recognition of mantric power can arise while listening to pop music, where rhythmic repetition of certain phrases—many of them fairly nonsensical in themselves—creates an observable effect on an audience. Sensitive individuals recognize the same effect in certain poetry, which often has the power to grip the mind in ways out of all proportion to the inherent meaning of the words. The scholar Robert Graves, himself no mean poet, went so far as to suggest that the only valid test of genuine poetry was whether it caused the hairs on the back of your neck to stand up.

In advanced meditation, the Tibetan mystic will typically cause all mental activity to cease—"dissolve his mind into nothingness," as one authority[74] puts it—then use an appropriate mantra to call from the void the force (or entity) with which he intends to unite. The precise rhythm and intonation will usually have been communicated to the practitioner by his or her guru, since these subtle inflections can never be apparent in the mantra's written form. It is, however, possible to

---

74. John Blofeld, an early translator of the Chinese I Ching.

achieve results through trial and error, although the time required may be daunting.

Although use of an apparently meaningless mantra (which in mystical Tibet may be repeated more than a thousand times at a single sitting) can strike the average Western reader as bizarre, the practice remains open to rational analysis. It can be argued that, properly used, a mantra is a more effective means of communication than, say, prayer. The very meaning of the prayer acts as a distraction to the mind and simultaneously limits thought to whatever is being said. A mantra, however, encourages concentration on what lies beyond the sound, unhindered by the limitations of meaning. As such, it can be—and undoubtedly is—a potent aid to meditation.

CHAPTER SIXTEEN

VOID MIND MEDITATION

Most of us are all too familiar with the chatter that goes on inside our own heads. We verbalize incessantly, talking mentally to ourselves from the moment we wake in the morning to the second we fall asleep at night. (Indeed, if you observe very closely, you'll discover yourself doing it even in dreams.)

The Irish author James Joyce famously portrayed this process in his classic novel *Ulysses,* attracting the literary description "stream of consciousness" as a result. For some, the verbal stream of consciousness is virtually the only mental activity they experience. There are even some who believe—contrary to the doctrines of Western psychology, it must be said—that verbal stream of consciousness, accompanied by the occasional daydream, actually *is* the mind as a whole.

Tibetan mystics and meditators disagree. At some time in the distant past, the Himalayan mystical tradition became interested in *margins*, those curious spaces where strange things seem to happen. It is in the margin between sleeping and waking—known in the West as the hypnogogic state—that many of us hear voices or experience hallucinations. It is in the wild hinterlands between settled human populations that ghosts are reputed to roam.

But for the Tibetans, the most important margin has long been the *space between thoughts.* However fleeting, there is an instant when one thought has ended and another has not yet arisen. This instant is the crack that permits Tibetan mystics to jimmy open the whole glorious experience of what's called *void mind* meditation.

This meditative process is deceptively simple for something that promises such profoundly far-reaching results. Leave aside half an hour each day for regular practice. Find a quiet spot where you won't be disturbed and sit with your spine straight. (Yoga practitioners assert, quite correctly, that cross-legged poses like the Lotus Pose or Perfect Pose influence your subtle energy flows in ways that help calm the mind. For the rest of us, who find such postures uncomfortable, excruciating, or impossible, a straight-backed chair will serve just as well.)

Establish your preparatory practices as given in the "Preparing to Meditate" section, then take a few preliminary moments to relax your body. Now half close your eyes and direct your gaze downward to a spot on the floor about five feet from where you are sitting. Then begin to count your breaths in groups of ten.

Breath control, like postures, forms an integral part of Hatha Yoga practice and can again be expected to have a profound influence on the mind. But the elegant simplicity of the Tibetan meditation form requires no breath control at all—only breath *observation*. Thus, you begin by noting your in-breath and counting "one," followed by your out-breath, counted as "two," the next in-breath, "three," and so on until you reach the out-breath "ten," at which point you begin again at "one."

There is no need to deepen your breathing, no need to force or change it in any way. Simply observe your breath and count—a process that is, in itself, remarkably calming. After a time, the counting becomes automatic, a sort of backdrop to your mental processes. Try to count your breaths and nothing more.

You won't succeed, of course.[75] However determinedly you attempt to hold to the simplicity of counting, extraneous thoughts

---

75. Unless you happen to be a very accomplished meditator.

will quickly intrude. This is only to be expected and should be no cause for concern. All you are required to do is make a mental note of the fact that you were temporarily distracted, then return to counting your breaths.

(If you are an organized personality, it may be useful to keep a diary record of your meditation practice, noting time of day, duration of session, and any distractions, problems, and so on, that may have arisen. This will allow you to keep track of your progress or lack of it. But do try to avoid turning the whole thing into a goal-oriented exercise aimed at achieving longer, deeper, better meditation. The "goal" of meditation is just to meditate.)

Even this simple exercise, performed regularly, brings considerable benefits. After a few weeks you will notice that your mind has become clearer. You will find that you are generally calmer and far less prone to negative thoughts and emotions. These are substantial compensations for what is, after all, no great effort. But you can, say the Tibetans, take things further.

Once meditation practice has become habitual, you may be encouraged to move toward void-mind itself—a process scarcely more complicated than the counting of your breaths.

Since this is—or will hopefully soon became—a spiritual exercise, it may be useful to begin by making a small offering in the form of a prayer, promise, or dedication—or perhaps simply light an incense cone—to whichever spiritual ideal your personal faith presents you. As a Christian, for example, you might make an offering to Jesus, or the Father God, or your favorite saint. As a Muslim, a dedication to Allah would clearly be more appropriate.

Tibetan Buddhists, like Buddhists everywhere, will generally make a threefold offering to their Three Jewels—the Buddha, the dharma (Buddhist teachings), and the sangha (the Community of Buddhist practice and priesthood). In offering to the Buddha, their minds turn toward Guatama's own enlightenment, which acts as a reminder that enlightenment is actually possible and hence encourages the effort needed to awaken. In offering to the dharma, they acknowledge the meaning that this body of truths has brought into their lives. In offering to the sangha, they seek the spiritual help of all Buddha's followers to guide them to a higher level of understanding. The more ambitious and confident among them might reiterate their determination to strive not only for their own enlightenment, but for the enlightenment of all conscious creatures—the praiseworthy goal of all Mahayana practitioners.

Whatever the conscious purpose of such offerings and to whom or what made, the act of offering something of yourself prior to void-mind meditation has the interesting psychological effect of loosening up a few of your more deeply embedded ideas about life, the world around you, and the nature of reality.

With the offering made, adopt your favored meditation position and, in a wholly receptive state, begin this time to observe your thoughts, not your breath. If you have previously practiced the counting meditation, you will probably already have noticed that thoughts no longer appear to be generated by you (whatever you believed before you took up meditation), but seem to arise of their own accord at the edges of your mind, then flow through your consciousness in associative streams.

As you observe your thoughts, try not to become involved in them. This may be difficult at first, since many intrusions carry their own emotional charge, but you can usually extricate yourself if you remember that the time to deal with the issues of daily life is after, not during, meditation practice.

Thoughts that are ignored quickly take their leave. True, they are just as quickly replaced by another stream, and then another, but be patient and keep watching. Eventually you will begin to notice that vitally important margin—the space between your thoughts.

At first the margin will be so brief it is scarcely more than an enticing flicker. But as your skill increases, the gaps become more frequent and, eventually, more expansive. Soon you will be able to examine them effectively. Tibetan mystics claim that when you do so, you will be staring into the Clear Light. The margins between thought, they say, contain the bedrock essence of your mind and the foundations of objective reality.

This easy equivalence of mind and reality runs completely contrary to Western conceptions, which differentiate between the subjective, which is internal, self-generated, and ephemeral, and the objective, which is external, independent, and, to all intents and purposes, eternal.

All the same, there are indications that our Western view may not be entirely correct and the doctrines of Tibetan mysticism may present clearer insights into the actual nature of reality.

Synesthesia is a condition in which the activation of one sense triggers a corresponding activation of another, so that synesthetes may be able to hear the sound of red or smell the scent of Sunday. The sensory cross-referencing can become complex: every word of the language may be experienced as having its own texture, sound, and shade; every note of a recital may evoke its own taste and smell. There can even be a hallucinatory element. Some synesthetes link numbers with spatial locations so that they appear to float in a line in the air, or experience one day of the week as somehow existing on their right, while another lies to their left.

For a long time, synesthesia was seen as a rare psychological aberration in much the same category as hearing voices. But recent research has suggested it is neither an aberration nor, indeed, all that rare. Scans of synesthetes show, for example, that when they claim to "hear" a particular color, there is simultaneous activity in both the visual cortex and auditory area of the brain. This means they literally *are* hearing colors, not hallucinating or imagining things.

The phenomenon arises from something analogous to cross-wiring. In what we think of as a "normal" brain, the various sites of sensory processing are quite separate. In a synesthete, some or all of them have neural links. Thus there is a "bleeding across" of sensation. The result is that the world is experienced differently.

The interesting thing is that tests have now shown that synesthesia is far more widespread than anyone ever suspected, but it's often at such a low level that it largely goes undetected, even by the synesthetes themselves. In fact, *you* may have it. When you describe your favorite singer as having a "dark brown voice," you may be expressing something more than metaphor: two separate areas of your brain may literally be lighting up.

The relevance of all of this to Tibetan ideas on mind and reality is that synesthesia is clearly not a disease, but simply a particular "wiring" of the brain that allows certain individuals to experience the world differently from their fellows. Yet some of that experience—like the layout of numbers floating in the air—does not seem "real" by any general criteria: the rest of us "know" that numbers don't float about like that.

But that knowledge arises purely from our sensory input, which in turn derives entirely from the way our brains are wired. Those of us who *fail* to see floating numbers actually lack the neural connections of the synesthete, and are consequently not unlike the inhabitants of the fictional Valley of the Blind, who concluded that their sighted visitors' experience of vision was a delusion caused by the curious protuberant growths that they called "eyes."

The logical conclusion reached from all this is that synesthetes, far from being ill or subnormal, are actually equipped to have a richer perception of reality than the rest of us. But this perception is wholly conditioned by the neural pathways of their brains, so it is equally valid to suggest that the differently-wired are engaged in *creating* a reality that is different from the reality created by you and me. Indeed, when we remember those floating numbers, the idea that the brain creates what we think of as external reality becomes quite appealing.

You can carry this insight far beyond the specialist studies into synesthesia. It is generally excepted that all our perceptions of the external world are filtered through our senses. But if rewiring our brains can enrich, rather than distort, those perceptions, then we are in the uncomfortable position of not knowing how far the creativity of our minds extends. It suddenly becomes reasonable to ask whether there anything at all "out there" or if we create it all. Western scientific studies have already confirmed that babies have to *learn* how to see: their eyes, although fully formed and fully functioning, are not "windows" on a pre-existent world.

In teaching our young the art of perception, then going on to teach them labels and language—this is a "tree," that is a "flower," over there is a "cat"—we create a consensus reality that quickly solidifies into an *unquestioned* consensus. It is something of a shock to discover that several surveys[76] show conclusively that people simply do not experience reality in exactly the same way,[77] as one would expect if reality itself were objective and external.

This is the precise position of Tibetan mysticism. What appears to be objective reality is an illusion, a transient dream maintained in its essentials only by a consensus of the unenlightened. The only permanent reality is mind.

But mind is not what you've always believed it to be.

---

76. Including a massive sampling currently being carried out by the BBC in Britain.

77. The differences are, however, buried under the weight of assumption. How often have you checked with the person beside you to see whether you are both seeing the same thing in every detail?

CHAPTER SEVENTEEN

IMPLICATIONS OF UNREALITY

Although it seems clear that Tibetan mystics reached their conclusions about the nature of reality experientially, their doctrine of the *void* is actually a restatement of the doctrine of maya propounded by the Indian founders of the Mahayana School in the fifth century AD. In Europe, centuries later, the Prussian philosopher Immanuel Kant came independently to a very similar position when he argued that time, space, and causation were not aspects of the external world, but rather categories the human mind imposed on the flow of events.

All the same, European philosophical thought has never quite come to grips with the implications of unreality in the way the Tibetans did. At the root of all Tibetan mysticism is the conviction that true enlightenment is impossible as long as the individual remains trapped in the illusion of duality, the hideously persistent notion that we exist as an ego consciousness *in here* while the world in all its diversity exists solidly and permanently *out there*. In Buddhism, neither the ego nor the world are real in any absolute sense. Only the fundamental mind exists, likened in the *Avatangsaka Sutra* to a bright mirror capable of reflecting all things so that phenomena like the ego and the world of appearances exist within it.

But this viewpoint, so fundamental to Mahayana Buddhism in general and Tibetan mysticism in particular, embodies a curious paradox. If the world is unreal and the ego-thing I believe to be me is unreal, why does morality matter? Why should I not lie, cheat, and steal to further my own ends, adopt a feel-good lifestyle fuelled by drugs and the exploitation of others? What possible difference could that make if it's all some sort of dream anyway?

The paradox is no light problem since Buddhism, as we shall see in a moment, is a profoundly moral religion, stressing right action almost above all else as the royal road to liberation. The Dalai Lama touched on it in 2003 when he gave instruction on the Six Paramitas to a two-thousand-strong Danish audience. The Six Paramitas are fundamental Buddhist practices that promise an increase in the happiness of your life while allowing you to transcend the bonds of illusion. Since they are based to a large degree on right actions, the path of the Paramitas neatly encompasses the paradox we have been discussing.

Clearly well aware of the problem, the Dalai Lama mentioned at an early stage of his lecture that certain Buddhist doctrines were relative rather than absolute, and included among them that most fundamental of all the Buddha's insights—that life is defined by suffering.

This stance is interesting since it implies that certain teachings and practices are necessary only in relation to an individual's level of spiritual development. It also points the way toward an understanding of the Tibetan emphasis on right action and attitude. On the basis of centuries of experience, Tibetan mystics believe that *wrong* action—lying, cheating, stealing—and *wrong* attitudes—hatred, envy, indifference to the suffering of others—all tend to solidify the illusion of ego. This bars access to the underlying void mind and consequently ensures that the individual never manages to see through the illusion of an external world.

The Dalai Lama has frequently emphasized that there is no single, exclusive, spiritual pathway. He believes that all religions can be helpful, and choice between them is largely a matter of individual temperament. This principle holds good *within* religions and can be applied to the various yogas, meditation techniques, and spiritual disciplines that make up the practice of Tibetan mysticism. While some are blessed with the application and self-discipline needed for void mind meditation, many are not.

But almost all are suited to the broad path of right action.

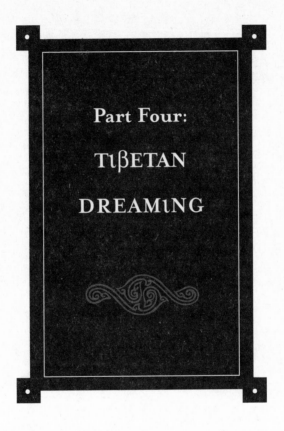

Part Four:

TιβETAN

DREAMιNG

CHAPTER EIGHTEEN

ROOTS OF THE DREAM

According to the ancient doctrines of Tibet, no dream is random. The mechanism of dreaming, which determines dream content, is related to the subtle rlung energies within the body.

Tibetans believe that your mind and energy system work in tandem. Energy is often described as a blind horse that has the potential to move about easily, but does not know where it is going. Mind, on the other hand, is seen as a lame rider—it can see where it might go, but is unable to travel to or, more importantly, remain in a particular place without great difficulty. The two together form a unit that functions a great deal more effectively than either would alone—but only when the rider learns to control the horse. When an untrained rider and horse get together, they often gallop far and wide, but usually without very much control over where they are going.

As you lose awareness of the physical world in the process of falling asleep, your mind is carried by the blind horse of rlung energy into a specific chakra. For the unenlightened, the goal chakra is absolutely determined by the karmic traces fixed within the energy itself. Each chakra is believed to be a doorway into one of the six realms we studied earlier,[78] possibly another way of saying that each chakra is associated with a particular level of consciousness.

The trigger that leads the mind to be drawn into a chakra is often something that happened to you during the day. You might, for example, have exchanged angry words with your spouse or suffered a bitter disappointment in love. The incident then activates an established karmic trace associated with the heart chakra. Thus, in sleep, your mind is drawn into that same chakra and the experience manifests as a dream.

Potentially, each dream provides an opportunity to deal with some aspect of your accumulated karma. Since Tibetans believe that dreams and waking consciousness are simply twin poles of the human mind, your reactions in a dream are just as capable of discharging karma, or laying down fresh karmic traces, as your reactions in waking life. Unfortunately, most of us remain ignorant of the spiritual possibilities presented by dreams, and incapable of taking advantage of them even if they were pointed out. For this reason, Tibetan dream yoga was developed. Among its aims is the centering of mind and rlung energy in the body's midline channel. If this can be achieved, dreaming becomes (relatively) free of personal karmic influences,[79] which permits the emergence of two new types of dreams. Tibetans call them dreams of clarity and Clear Light dreams.

Dreams of clarity are essentially knowledge dreams. As you become increasingly proficient in dream yoga, your dreams become clearer, more vivid and detailed. Such dreams are not (necessarily) lucid, but they tend to be more easily remembered and do represent an increased awareness of the dream state. You will already know how, in ordinary dreams, you can be swept from one scene to another, one experience to another, with little rhyme or reason. Everything is fluid and shifting, nearly impossible to follow in any rational way. Dreams of clarity are far more stable, and you are far more stable within them, reflecting the fact that the blind horse and lame rider have ceased to

---

78. Hell, hungry ghost, animal, human, demi-god, and god.

79. Although not, as we shall see, free of collective karma.

be buffeted by personal karmic winds, but have emerged from the chakras to take refuge in the central channel.

In dreams of clarity, you are still presented with images and experiences, but the information embodied in them is no longer the result of your personal karma. It is drawn instead from a transpersonal source. Such dreams may offer teachings from divine beings or dream representations of your guru, and as such may become a useful guide to your spiritual practice. Dreams of clarity do not, however, embody the ultimate experience of illumination, since collective karma, largely generated by your cultural environment, remains in operation and maintains the illusion of duality.

Although a dream of clarity can arise for anyone, the experience is rare until you become proficient in dream yoga. Tibetan masters warn that not all dreams that present the appearance of spiritual guidance are necessarily dreams of clarity. If you have an interest in esoteric matters (and have perhaps just begun some form of spiritual practice), it is very natural that you might dream of such things. But dreams of this sort, which arise before mind and rlung energies become stable, are almost always driven by karma, and the doctrines they present shift and change with the activation of each new karmic trace.

You may have encountered people who have become victims of karmic "knowledge" dreams. They seem to be incapable of making the simplest decision without some form of "spirit guidance." Keeping up with orders from their "inner contacts" becomes a full-time occupation. They become locked in a personal drama of their own manufacture and see signs and portents everywhere. Their only real hope is to develop discrimination and learn to separate the rare dreams that contain genuine spiritual wisdom from the many that arise from personal fantasies.

Clear Light dreams can take a decade or more of yoga practice to emerge since they arise out of the pristine rlung energy in the central channel untainted by any karmic trace. They are of two types. One can scarcely be called a dream at all since it involves a nondual state of voidness free from images or even thought. The other is more difficult to describe since mental activities—including dream images—continue to manifest, but the individual has ceased to experience them in dualist terms. Because ego has vanished, thoughts and images are no longer seen as somehow "out there" with the individual as an observer. Rather, everything—that which is experienced and the individual experiencing it—becomes a seamless whole.

If you are familiar with Oriental doctrines, you may have noted the similarities between the Clear Light dream state and states of mystical ecstasy, or even enlightenment. This is by no means accidental. Tibetans refer to the experience of nonduality as *rigpa*—an enlightened state in which the individual at long last realizes that there is no boundary between him or her and the whole of manifest existence; all is everything, all is unity, and the only ultimate reality is that of the Clear Light void.

Various yogas are designed to spark such a realization, leaving their practitioners in increasingly long periods of rigpa. But since dreaming and waking consciousness are simply two aspects of the same mind, the development of the rigpa state during the day leads inevitably to Clear Light (rigpa) dreaming at night. Conversely, the practice of dream yoga, which leads to a Clear Light dream, will tend to stimulate the experience of rigpa during the daytime.

CHAPTER NINETEEN

DREAM YOGA

The whole of Tibetan dream yoga is driven by a realization that karmic traces tend to lock us into a state of ignorance. In order to break the lock, we need to become constantly aware of how we generate—and regenerate—karmic traces. This awareness enables us to break the habits of several lifetimes and cultivate nonattachment.

Clearly, the more time you devote to your efforts, the sooner you will get results. Tibetans, a superlatively pragmatic people, long ago decided that since we spend approximately a third of our lives asleep, it made good sense to develop a "Practice of the Night." It gives you more time to engage in spiritual disciplines and does not interfere with a practicalities of daily life. (Although the ultimate goal might be a Clear Light in which all opposites are reconciled, we have to live in a dualistic world until we get there. So things like earning a living are important.)

But in order to practice spiritual disciplines while you are asleep, you need to be aware of your current state, otherwise there is no possibility of control over what you do. The most advanced yogic masters actually manage to retain conscious awareness throughout the entire sleep state—something almost incomprehensible to Western science. The rest settle for conscious awareness during dreams. In other words, lucid dreaming.

The Tibetan system for achieving (then going beyond) lucidity differs from the various Western techniques already examined. It embodies the familiar platforms of Tibetan occultism: sonics, visualization, mind control, and manipulation of the rlung energies. Since the successful dream yogi must have sufficient control to avoid being swept away in the tidal wave of karmic traces that typically manifest in dreams, the practice begins not with dreamwork at all, but with a particular meditation designed to stabilize the mind. The meditation is known as "calm abiding," *zhiné* in Tibetan, and is virtually identical to the Western religious practice of contemplation. The technique begins with the mind fixed on a single object and develops over time to a stage when the mind can be held fixed without the need for an objective focus. The three stages of the practice are known as Forceful Zhiné, Natural Zhiné, and Ultimate Zhiné.

Although calm abiding can use any object when practiced for its own sake, as a preparation for dream yoga, Tibetan gurus often suggest the use of the Tibetan letter *A*, which looks like this:

Make up a meditation card. Although the card itself may be square, it should contain five concentric circles. The innermost, just over an inch in diameter, is to be indigo, the next blue, the next green, then red, yellow, and white. In the center circle, carefully paint the Tibetan letter *A* so it emerges white out of the indigo background. Now fix the card to a rod long enough to place it at eye level when you are seated cross-legged. Attach the rod to a base.

To begin your practice, you require to be seated in a comfortable cross-legged posture with your hands folded in your lap, palms upward, one on top of the other. Hold your spine straight, but not rigid, and tuck your chin in to straighten your neck. Set your card-stand in front of you about eighteen inches away from your eyes. If you have made it correctly, you should be able to look at the card without raising or lowering your eyes. Let your eyes relax; keeping them neither wide open nor shut. Breathe normally and fix your gaze on the object. Remain quite still and try to focus your concentration exclusively on the white Tibetan *A*.

You will find this extremely difficult at first, especially if you have limited experience with meditation. Your mind will tend to slide away to think of other things. You will be distracted by any movement or noise around you, but each time you experience a distraction, bring your mind back to the card. After a few moments, you will quickly realize why this is called the stage of Forceful Zhiné. The practice is only possible if you keep forcing your mind back time and again to the object of your contemplation. In the early stages, it can be quite helpful to take frequent breaks rather than attempting one long meditative session, but even during breaks try to remember that this is purely a short, temporary rest from a difficult spiritual practice.

What you are attempting is the exact mental equivalent of exercising a muscle. You have to keep at it if you want results. Push against your limits and, with time, the mental muscle will grow progressively stronger.

As you gaze at the object of your contemplation, try not to think about it. If you find yourself engaged in an inner dialogue ("This is the letter *A* in Tibetan," "It's an interesting shape," and so on), then you are falling short of your goal. What you want is a simple, present-moment *awareness* of the letter; no more and no less. Allow your breathing to calm until you are no longer aware of it. Allow your body to relax. Allow your mind to sink deeper and deeper into a state of calm and peace, but guard against falling asleep or into trance.

At this stage, and perhaps even at later stages, you may find yourself subject to unusual physical sensations. These are a natural outcome of what you are trying to do—the mind resists training and will distract you if it can!—and can be ignored.

With practice, things will become easier. You will find that the periods of time spent free of mind-wandering become progressively longer until, suddenly, you will be able to contemplate the symbol on the card without having to force your attention back again and again. You have entered the stage of Natural Zhiné.

At this point you can embark on a very interesting experiment. Try to achieve the same mental state without the symbol. Put away the card and see if you can focus your attention on empty space. An expanse of clear sky is probably best as something to look at, but any area of space will do. Remember, you are not trying to focus on a point within this space, but on the space itself. Stay calm and relaxed and allow your mind to diffuse throughout the whole of the space you are contemplating (Tibetans call this "dissolving the mind"—a wonderfully expressive description of the experience).

When you dissolve the mind successfully, you enter the third stage of the exercise, Ultimate Zhiné. You may or may not recognize your achievement. (If you were a student in Tibet, your guru would alert you.) It is not characterized by any dramatic transition, but rather by a certain ease and lightness. You will find that your thoughts arise and then dissolve without effort or influence. Look carefully—this is something else your guru would have pointed out to you—and you will be able to differentiate between the *functioning* of your mind in the form of thoughts or pictures, and the steady, unvarying *presence* of the mind itself.

Properly directed, Zhiné practice alone can take you a long way on the mystic path, but for many practitioners, it is the initial step toward the fascinating experiences of dream yoga. The first practice of dream yoga itself involves an attempt to reduce the chaos of the typical dream state by making some changes in your karmic traces. The method used to do this is similar to the Western lucid dream practice of reality testing, but with one very important difference.

In the West, prospective lucid dreamers embark on a (waking) regime that involves their stopping from time to time to make sure they are truly awake. As reality testing becomes habitual, the theory is that they will begin to carry out the same instinctive tests while asleep. Once they do, it is easy to determine that they are actually dreaming, and the dream itself goes lucid.

Westerners engaged in this practice take it for granted that there is an essential difference between the waking state and the dream. Awake, you function in the real world; dreaming, you don't. The distinction is not nearly so clear cut for Tibetans. Thus, the "reality check" of the West, designed to differentiate between waking reality and dreaming illusion, is replaced by an "unreality check," designed to remind you that asleep or awake, *everything* you experience is an illusion. Tibetan dream gurus advise that throughout your waking day, you continually remind yourself that you are living in a dream. The car you drive is a dream car. The building where you work is a dream building. The money you make is dream money. All appearances are creations of your mind.

It is not enough to simply keep repeating, "This is all a dream." You need to make the effort to feel it in your bones, to realize the profound truth you are expressing. Use your imagination and anything else that helps. Oddly enough, this practice does not turn your waking world into a shimmering heat mirage, but rather makes it more vivid and gives you a greater sense of presence—signs that you are properly engaged with your spiritual work and have not sunk into habitual repetition.

The focus of the technique needs to be as much on yourself as on your environment. After all, if everything is a dream, then you are the dreamer. But that means you are dreaming the body with indigestion and arthritis, the anger at your boss, the disappointment with your children. You are also, let it be said, dreaming the lust that possesses you, the pleasure of friendship, the happiness you sometimes feel when facing a new dawn. All these things, which you have believed for a lifetime to be your very essence, are no more than the creations of your mind.

As you engage in the practice, a change occurs in your outlook. You begin to realize that everything happening is both transient and intimately related to the projections of your mind. This inevitably changes your reaction to events—something which, in the past, has been largely unconscious anyway. Life has less power over you since you are no longer handing your own power over to it. You may recall the Tibetan belief that karmic traces are generated by reactions rather than experiences or even actions. Against this background, it follows that in changing your reactions by coming to recognize the illusory quality of life, you will tend to generate fewer karmic traces. The karmic change leads in turn to a change in dream content.

(Although not part of Tibetan dream yoga theory, it is easy to see how the habitual questioning of the reality of your waking state must sooner or later lead to your questioning the nature of your dream state. Once the pertinent question is asked, lucidity follows.)

A consequence of the "unreality check"—seen by Tibetans as a separate stage of the practice—is a decrease in both desire and aversion. Letting go in this way is a powerful antidote to depression, anger, envy, and other unhappy states.

The next stage of dream yoga involves a variation on a technique that will be familiar to some Western occultists—the evening review. The evening review is itself a very simple exercise. You are required go over the events of the day immediately before you fall asleep, simply recalling each one without passion or judgment. In the Tibetan variation, you are urged to view your recollections as memories of dreams. Use your intellect to comprehend this fully—any memory shares many characteristics with a dream, after all—and try to see the projections that sustained your experiences. It is very useful to note the differences that arise when you relate to an experience as a dream and when you relate to it as something real and solid.

When you complete your review, focus your intent on recognizing the events of the night for the dreams they are. Tibetan gurus see this as "sending a wish," and this viewpoint too can be useful. Try to experience your intent as a prayer to your inner teachers or gods, promising to do your best to recognize the true nature of your dreams and asking their help in the endeavor.

In the morning, you should make an effort to remember the dreams of the night. This may not be easy at first, and it is perfectly permissible to leave a notebook or tape recorder beside your bed so you can make notes. As you recall your dreams, see them for the illusions they were and determine to recognize the illusory quality of your experiences in the coming day.

Taken together, these techniques follow a twenty-four-hour Wheel of Spiritual Practice aimed at convincing you that both your inner and your outer worlds have the essence of maya.

CHAPTER TWENTY

SLEEP YOGA

Tibetan mystics take sleep seriously. They believe that purifying the mind before retiring for the night generates greater presence in dreams, reduces karmic influences, and ensures a more positive experience altogether. A purified mind is particularly important should you embark on the path of dream yoga. One way of achieving it is known as the "Nine Purifications Breathing."

This exercise is based on the observation that stress influences the way you breathe. Tibetans long ago decided to find out whether the reverse was true—that the way you breathe might influence your stress levels. They discovered that it was true, and developed the Nine Purifications Breathing as a result.

Begin by sitting cross-legged in your usual meditation position, spine straight but not rigid, chin tucked in to straighten your neck, and hands placed palms up in your lap, left hand on top of your right.

Now visualize the three major channels of energy within your body (the rtsa, discussed in chapter 2). For this exercise there is no need to visualize the chakras; concentrate instead on picturing the channels clearly. Establish the central channel first. It is roughly the thickness of a bamboo cane and runs through the center of your body, widening a little from the level of your heart to the crown of your head. It is clear blue in color.

When you can see the central channel clearly in your mind's eye, turn your attention to the two side channels. These are narrower than the central channel, about the diameter of a pencil. These channels curve round to join with the center channel at the base of your body, some four inches below your navel. They rise parallel to the center channel on either side, and curve up over the skull and down behind the eyes to form a complete circuit. Some authorities note that they have openings as the nostrils, indicating the close relationship between the breath and the body's subtle energies.

Like the central channel, each of the the side channels has a distinctive color, but this differs depending on your sex. If you are male, the channel in the right side of your body is white, while that in the left side is red. If you are female, the colorings are reversed—your right channel is red and the left is white. This difference in channel coloring is reflected in slight variations in the Nine Purifications technique, which also depends on whether you are a man or a woman.

Although most practices—including this one—concentrate on the three major energy channels, there are, in fact, a great many other energy flows throughout your body. The various yoga postures and hand gestures, called *mudras*, are designed to influence these flows in subtle ways. There is a simple mudra involved in the Nine Purifications: pressing your thumb against the base of your ring finger.

To begin the exercise proper, follow this sequence:

Men

1. Press your right thumb against the base of your right ring finger. Raise your right hand and close off your right nostril with the ring finger. Inhale green light through your left nostril. Now close off your left nostril (again using your right ring finger) and exhale completely through the right nostril. As you exhale, imagine that you expel all masculine problems and obstacles from the white channel. As you do so, the air you exhale should be visualized as turning light blue. This represents one Purification. Repeat the process until you have completed three rounds of inhalation and exhalation.

2. Change hands and complete another three rounds of inhala-
    tion and exhalation exactly as before, but using the opposite
    nostril. Each time you exhale, imagine that you are expelling
    all feminine problems and obstacles from the red channel. As
    you do so, the air you exhale should be visualized as turning
    pale pink. This completes six of the Nine Purifications.

3. Ensure that your left hand is on top of your right, palm upward
    in your lap. Inhale green light into both nostrils. Imagine it as a
    healing balm moving down the two side channels until it
    reaches the junction with the center channel at the base. On
    your out-breath, visualize the light moving up the center chan-
    nel to emerge from the top of your head. As you do so, imagine
    all problems and illnesses associated with malevolent spirits
    expelled from the top of your head in the form of black smoke.
    Three rounds of this practice complete the Nine Purifications.

Women

1. Press your left thumb against the base of your left ring finger.
    Raise your left hand and close off your left nostril with the ring
    finger. Inhale green light through your right nostril. Now close
    off your right nostril (again using your left ring finger) and
    exhale completely through the left nostril. As you exhale,
    imagine that you expel all masculine problems and obstacles
    from the white channel. As you do so, the air you exhale should
    be visualized as turning light blue. This represents one Purifica-
    tion. Repeat the process until you have completed three rounds
    of inhalation and exhalation.

2. Change hands and complete another three rounds of inhalation
    and exhalation exactly as before, but using the opposite nostril.
    Each time you exhale, imagine that you are expelling all femi-
    nine problems and obstacles from the red channel. As you do
    so, the air you exhale should be visualized as turning pale pink.
    This completes six of the Nine Purifications.

3. Ensure that your left hand is on top of your right, palm upward in your lap. Inhale green light into both nostrils. Imagine it as a healing balm moving down the two side channels until it reaches the junction with the center channel at the base. On your out-breath, visualize the light moving up the center channel to emerge from the top of your head. As you do so, imagine all problems and illnesses associated with malevolent spirits expelled from the top of your head in the form of black smoke. Three rounds of this practice complete the Nine Purifications.

After the Nine Purifications, you can get into bed and begin the exercises designed to get your dreams in order and, eventually, trigger lucidity. Perhaps the simplest of them is as follows:

Take a few deep breaths to calm and steady yourself, then focus your concentration on visualizing a white representation of the letter *A* in the center of your body. Since the letter must be associated with its relevant sound—*ahhh*—you may prefer to use the English letter *A*, although this obviously does not figure in the original Tibetan texts. Like many esoteric practices, this variation can be approached in the spirit of trial and error: if it works for you, use it. Purists, however, will prefer the original Tibetan symbol:

Whether English *A* or Tibetan ཨ, bear in mind that both symbols represent the same *ahhh* sound. Hear that sound in your mind as uttered from the symbol itself.

Try to focus your mind on the symbol for as long as possible, but if this proves difficult, it is worth realizing that the important point is to have the symbol mentally in place *as you fall asleep.* Should you find yourself in difficulties with a static visualization, try imagining that a second symbol emerges from the first, then a third from the second, until a chain of them reaches from your heart area all the way up to the crown of your head. Now, symbol by symbol, see the chain retreat back down until there is a single central symbol once more. Repeat this process until you fall asleep. Although it sounds difficult, it actually has a soporific effect, rather like the famous "counting sheep."

The real trick, however, is to practice until the whole process becomes instinctive. When you reach that stage, you no longer feel you are visualizing the imaginal symbol, but rather calling it up. Once this is achieved, the symbol will persist with no effort on your part. Consequently, you can relax completely and allow yourself to move into the sleep state with both your concentration and the symbol itself intact. Correctly performed, the exercise leads to lucidity, although this is seen as a secondary effect. The main goal is to balance the energies in the central channel, and, consequently, you are advised to re-establish the symbol and sound the *ahhh* immediately on wakening.

A more complex practice with essentially the same goal begins by advising you to lie in a particular way as you prepare for sleep. Men should lie on their right side, women on their left, both with their head in the north. Draw up your knees a little to give stability to the position, rest your head in the palm of your underneath hand, and leave your upper arm straight along your body. Relax and calm your breathing until it is no longer audible.

Visualize a red, four-petaled lotus at the position of your throat chakra. Mentally place a luminous Tibetan *A*— ཨ —at its center and note how the symbol picks up the color of the petals. Visualize the

Tibetan syllables *Ra, Sha, La,* and *Sa,* respectively, at front, back, left, and right of each petal. The appearance of these syllables is:

ཪ་   ཤ་   ལ་   ས་

Ra   **Sha**   **La**   **Sa**

Keep your mind focused on the central ཨ *(A)* as you fall asleep. Sleep for two hours—set the alarm clock if necessary—then move on to the next part of the practice. Get back into your initial sleeping position (if you are not still in it), then inhale and gently hold your breath. Clench the muscles of your pelvic floor so there is a sensation of pushing the breath upward to compress it just below the navel. Hold your breath for a few seconds longer, then release it while simultane- ously relaxing all the muscles of your body, including those of the chest and pelvic floor.

As you engage in the breathing exercise, bring your attention to your third eye, the brow chakra located just above the point where your eyebrows meet. Visualize a small, luminous ball of white light there. Try to feel the ball as if it were physically there.

At first, your efforts will be expended simply on the visualization, but as happened with previous visualizations, there will come a time when this one becomes automatic and requires no effort to hold. When this happens, you can begin to allow your mind to merge with the light from this little sphere, becoming increasingly clear. You will find that this stage of the exercise not only stimulates lucid dreams, but can actually help you maintain a continuity of consciousness between waking and sleeping states.

---

80. In Tibet, the traditional time to begin sleep yoga is 10 p.m. This means that the second stage of the practice coincides with midnight, while the third occurs some two hours before dawn. Although the timing here does not appear to be critical, it does suggest that the Tibetan dream sages were well aware of their natural dream patterns.

The next part of the practice comes two hours after the last.[80] Once more you should awaken (with the alarm clock if necessary), but this time you need to adopt a new sleeping position. Stack your pillows high and lie on your back with your legs loosely crossed, knees bent, so that if you were to sit up you would move into a loose semblance of a meditation posture.

Bring your attention to your heart chakra and visualize the Tibetan syllable *Hung* there. The syllable looks like this:

You should imagine it as black, but luminous. Begin a sequence of twenty-one deep breaths, taken without strain, and allow your consciousness to merge with the *Hung* syllable. Fall asleep in the merged state.

Although the fourth part of this practice is traditionally carried out two hours after the third and immediately before the first light of a Tibetan dawn, it is actually just as effective if you allow yourself to waken naturally. If you are anything like I am first thing in the morning, you will be relieved to hear there are no special positions or breathing exercises. Instead, you should simply get comfortable and focus your attention on your base chakra between your genitals and anus. Visualize a black luminous sphere[81] at that point, and again let your consciousness merge with it. Once you have done so, allow yourself to fall asleep again for a final period of cozy dreaming before you finally get up to face your working day.

Except, that is, your dreams—in this period at least—may be anything but cozy. All four stages of the practice are designed to manipulate your energies in ways that produce specific *types* of dreams.

The first, pre-sleep practice, has the effect of generating peaceful, gentle dreams.

---

81. The paradox involved in a luminous black object is less acute in the imaginal realm, as you will see as soon as you attempt the visualization.

The second practice, two hours later, carries the promise of transition consciousness and increased luminosity in the dream process, but even before that happens you should experience symbols of progress in the dream itself. Your dreams will suggest you are moving toward something, and should be bright and enjoyable.

The third practice, involving the *Hung* syllable, aims to develop your power—specifically to put you in touch with the pre-existent power you have within yourself. With the contact comes a sense of security, and the dreams generated reflect this. You may well find yourself in positions of authority or the object of approval from your peers.

The final practice tends to produce dreams that are far less pleasant, but just as important. The Tibetans refer to them as "wrathful," and you may find yourself overwhelmed by storms or floods or any one of a multitude of aggressive forces. In the West, dreams of this type are classified as nightmares, and we do our best to forget them as quickly as possible. For the Tibetan dream yogi, they are opportunities to develop the quality of fearlessness.

Such a development naturally arises when you realize that however often your dream self is destroyed by the horrors of a wrathful dream, it somehow miraculously survives intact. The lesson is in many ways similar to the experience of the Rite of Chöd, in which you permit yourself to be utterly devoured, yet endure. Familiarity with wrathful dreams will bring not contempt, but a realization of the fact that, ultimately, nothing can actually harm you. This realization is, of course, intimately linked with the understanding that your sleeping environment, however solid it may seem, however terrifying it may appear, is nothing but a dream and hence the product of your own mind. In short, it is linked with lucidity.

Although lucidity is not the ultimate goal of Tibetan dream yoga, it is certainly a vital tool that the Tibetan masters work hard to develop. Without lucidity, you are condemned to accept the illusion of reality all dreams present. With it, you can begin to make real spiritual progress. An ancient Tantric text gives this advice to those who achieve lucidity:

At the outset, in the process of realizing it to be maya (illusion) abandon all feeling of fear; And, if the dream be of fire, transform the fire into water, the antidote of fire. And if the dream be of minute objects, transform them into large objects; Or if the dream be of large objects, transform them into small objects: Thereby one comprehendeth the nature of dimensions. And if the dream be of a single thing, transform it into many things; Or if the dream be of many things, transform them into a single thing: Thereby one comprehendeth the nature of plurality and of unity.[82]

There are two reasons why the Tibetan practitioners seek this degree of dream control—one associated with life, the other with death.

Toward the end of the seventeenth century, the self-styled "foolish monk" Lochen Dharma Shri had this to say about the development of dream lucidity:

Apprehending the Dreams
During the daytime, sustaining mindfulness without distraction
Apart from the power of mental imprints, phenomena do not exist.
All avenues of appearances, negative and affirmative,
Are dreamlike, though they are apprehended as external phenomena.
Without distraction, earnestly and continually sustain your mindfulness
And attention to this truth.[83]

---

82. Quoted by W. Y. Evans-Wentz in *Tibetan Yoga and Secret Doctrines* (Oxford: Oxford University Press, 1969).

83. Quoted in *Ancient Wisdom*, by the Venerable Gyatrul Rinpoche (New York: Snow Lion Publications, 1993).

This, as you can see, is a succinct expression of the techniques examined earlier, designed to trigger lucidity by cultivating the mental habit of seeing your waking experience as a dream. Once the habit is ingrained, it will be carried into the dream state and lucidity results.

But Lochen's advice goes beyond this. The real thrust of dream yoga is to demonstrate *by experience* the truth of the Buddhist doctrine of maya, the same truth realized by those who doubt the reality of their yidam. When you become lucid in a dream, your dream environment appears no less real, no less solid, no less detailed. Indeed, if anything, the dream will often become more vivid than before. Yet simply by comprehending its actual nature, you can change it in any way you wish. You can, as the Tantric text states, change fire into water, turn large objects into small.

When you have done this a few times, it is almost inevitable that you will develop some deep reservations about the reality of your waking world. The idea that your daylight existence might also be an illusion is no longer an intellectual exercise designed to create the right mindset for lucid dreaming at night. Instead, it gradually becomes a bred-in-the-bone conviction.

And here, although it is seldom spelled out to the uninitiated, is the single, central secret of Tibetan magic. If waking reality is a dream, then surely it can be manipulated just like the sleep dreams of the night. All that is really required is awareness of the truth.

With mastery of dream yoga comes the potential to change your waking circumstances at will. If the world is maya, an illusion generated by your mind, then manipulation of your mind can change the nature of the illusion. As in your sleeping dreams, you can do anything you want—raise storms, change lead into gold, walk on water . . . all the astonishing talents attributed to magicians in every culture down the ages.

It is no coincidence that virtually every system of magic on the face of this planet is based on two basic premises: that you can do anything you *believe* you can do, and that clear, detailed visualization of a result will tend to bring that result about. Certainly for all the para-phernalia of ritual practice and talk of astral energies, these twin prin-ciples underlie the whole of the Western Esoteric Tradition. The train-ing, trappings, and techniques serve only to support them. In the West, there is no clear theory about why magical methods should work, only the experience that—in certain hands—they do.

Yet magic, as anyone who has attempted its practice will confirm, is erratic; an art rather than a science. Without the basis of a valid the-ory, it is difficult to understand why. From Tibet, the answer comes swooping in. Basic belief in yourself and visualization of results will achieve results in direct proportion to your degree of realization that the world around you is unreal, the product of your mind.

Changing the dream for good or ill is a great temptation, but ulti-mately it is a mug's game. The world's most powerful sorcerer, whether saint or sinner, comes inevitably to face the futility of his existence at the moment of death. And this brings us directly to the second reason why Tibetan masters seek to practice dream control.

For those like Saint Milarepa, who abandoned the magical path and sought instead to follow the mystical way, dream yoga has become an extraordinarily effective compass for negotiating the after-death state to achieve enlightenment and liberation from the wheel of birth, death, and rebirth. The "foolish monk" Lochen describes the process thus:

> *The absorption of unification with the bardo state*
> *If, during the night, you familiarise yourself with the inseparability*
> *Of the illusory body, the dream and the bardo state*
> *Imagine the play of the spiritual body through the gradual dissolution*
> *Into the ultimate clear light of death.*
> *Imagine all self-arising deceptive appearances*
> *As the arisings of the illusory fulfilled body.*

> *Attend to the emptiness and lack of true existence of the*
> *entrance ways*
> *And thus train in the ways of the emanation body.*[84]

Although the language is a little obscure in parts, the overall thrust of the instruction is clear enough. Lochen Dharma Shri is advising his readers to practice for death, to stage a rehearsal in advance of the actual event. Dream yoga is the perfect way to do so, since dreaming shares so many characteristics with the bardo state.

What Lochen is saying here is that by examining the mechanics of dreaming itself while in a lucid dream, you can come to understand how your dream body, your dream environment, and the underlying structure of your mind are all one and the same thing—body and environment are simply mental projections. This done, you can use the lucid dream to familiarize yourself with an experience you must undergo one day—your own death.

---

84. Quoted, with minor changes, from *Ancient Wisdom,* by the Venerable Gyatrul Rinpoche (New York: Snow Lion Publications, 1993).

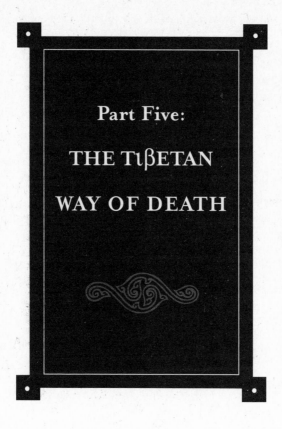

Part Five:

THE TιβETAN

WAY OF DEATH

CHAPTER TWENTY-ONE

THE DEADLY ART OF
LIVING WELL

Western attitudes toward death generally involve some degree of denial. Although well aware intellectually that you and I must die one day, we routinely live our lives as if it were never going to happen. Those in their late eighties and nineties continue cheerfully to make plans for their next year's holidays and accept dinner invitations while prey to serious illnesses. Death is seldom discussed in polite company. The subject is considered morbid.

Our "scientific" view of death, which in all conscience should be one of agnosticism, routinely teaches that death equates with annihilation and loss, leading to emotions of fear on the rare occasions when we do speak about it.

Even when death actually occurs, denial continues. The practice of embalming is so widespread in the United States that many people believe (wrongly) it is a legal requirement. Unknown to most people (who prefer not to think about the work of our busy undertakers), embalming involves the insertion of a tube into the large blood vessel leading into the heart, or into the heart itself. Then, using a suction apparatus, the undertaker draws off as much blood as possible. Draining a corpse is no easy job, even with mechanical help. To facilitate the process, a chemical mixture of formaldehyde, glycerin, borax, phenol, potassium nitrate, acetate, saffranin, methyl red, and water is pumped into the body under pressure via a vein in the armpit. This mixture is commonly called *embalming fluid*, and each ingredient has a specific purpose. Formaldehyde preserves the tissues. Glycerin stops dehydration. Borax liquifies the blood. Phenol, potassium nitrate, and acetate are all disinfectants. Saffranin and methyl red are dyes. They effect skin tone and give the cadaver a pleasingly lifelike appearance.

Which is, of course, the whole object of the exercise. Anyone who takes the trouble to investigate will quickly discover that embalming does not, as commonly believed, preserve a body in perpetuity. An embalmed corpse will always disintegrate in time. Unless it's buried somewhere bone dry, like the Egyptian Desert, the process won't even take very long. The *only* real result of embalming is to make the corpse look presentable—that is, healthy but asleep—to the next of kin. In short, funeral practice conspires to assist in the emotional denial of death.[85]

There is, of course, a minority in the West who are prepared to look death in the eye, so to speak, concluding that it is both inevitable and natural, and, consequently, not worth worrying about—an attitude described by the Tibetan spiritual leader Chagdud Tulku Rinpoche as "all very well until you are actually dying."

Denial of death, its equation with annihilation, and the mindless assumption that your own death will, as a natural process, somehow work out all right for you, combine to rob life of any sense of meaning and block the development of a long-term attitude toward the world's main problems. As the former Brazilian Minister of the Environment, Jose Antonio Lutzenberger, remarked in 1991, we act as if we were the last generation on the planet, systematically dismantling life-support systems like the ozone layer and oxygen-producing forests, while simultaneously poisoning rivers, oceans, and atmosphere.

The Tibetan attitude toward death presents a sharp contrast. To begin with, Tibetans accept, almost without question,[86] the doctrine

---

85. Denial of death is far-reaching. When I wrote a book on the topic some years ago, several publishers declined it on the grounds that they "didn't like to think about the subject."

of reincarnation. This belief is absolutely ingrained in their culture—to such a degree, in fact, that prior to the Chinese invasion, it was possible for a Tibetan to take out a loan in this life, repayable in the next. Neither the borrower nor the lender saw anything odd in the arrangement. A belief of this type encourages the long view, if only from selfish motives. There is a great deal to be said for preserving the planet if you are likely to be reborn on it.

But Tibetan mystics go further. In the Buddhist view, life and death are aspects of a whole. One teacher has described death as "a mirror in which the entire meaning of life is reflected." In practical terms, Buddhist doctrine assures you that it is perfectly possible to prepare for death, in a wholly meaningful way, during your lifetime. By doing so, you literally prepare yourself for the experience of death, the chain of reincarnations beyond it, and, hopefully, for the eventual liberated enlightenment that gives access to the Clear Light.

The preparation—itself a lifetime's work—is based on two intertwined premises:

1. It is certain you will die.
2. It is uncertain when, where, and how you will die.

It seems to be a fundamental quirk of human nature to seize on the second premise as an excuse to avoid facing the first. This leads to a state sometimes referred to as "active laziness." The controversial Tibetan guru Soygal Rinpoche retells a traditional story from his homeland to illustrate the meaning of active laziness:

A totally impoverished Tibetan embarked on a program of hard, relentless, backbreaking work until, after many months, he managed to accumulate a whole sack of grain. The sack represented more wealth than he'd ever had in his life, and when he got home, he used a strong rope to hang it from the rafters of his house to make sure it was safe from rats and thieves. As an added precaution, he decided to sleep underneath it.

---

86. But not blindly. When the reincarnation of a Dalai Lama is sought, for example, pains are taken to find proof of the rebirth.

One night he began to plan his life. He was proud of his capacity for hard work, proud of what he had already done, but he knew deep in his heart he could do even better. He decided that rather than selling the sack as a whole, he would divide the grain into smaller quantities and sell each packet off for a bigger profit margin. This would allow him not only to buy food, but it would leave enough money for him to invest in more grain.

With a second sack of grain, he could repeat the process and continue to reinvest the profits until he became rich and achieved some real standing in his community. Once that happened, there would be lots of women who would want to marry him and he would pick the most beautiful. Soon a child would come along, the son he'd always wanted.

He began to cast around for a name for the child. At that point he noticed the moon rising through the little window of his room and at once decided this was a favorable omen. "I'll call him 'As Famous As the Moon!'" he exclaimed.

At which point the rope broke and the bag of grain fell on his head, killing him instantly.

The story not only illustrates the Tibetan love of gallows humor, but carries as important message for the West in particular. There are two distinct kinds of laziness. One consists of staying in bed until noon, then lounging around all day, telephoning friends and listening to pop music.[87] But the other, which is something of a way of life in developed countries like America, consists of packing the day so full of compulsive "responsibilities" that no time is left to confront— indeed even recognize—the real issues. In the words of one Tibetan master, "You are housekeeping in a dream."

And it's a dream from which you may wake up at any moment.

The Tibetan word for *body* is *lu,* which translates literally as "something you must leave behind." Realizing this, Tibetan mystics are no more concerned with physical comforts and improving their

---

87. Readers with teenage children may recognize the pattern.

life than we would be with redecorating a motel room where we happened to be staying overnight. "You have to eat, sleep, and excrete," remarked Patrul Rinpoche. "Beyond that, it's none of your business."

Another master with the same mindset, Gyalse Rinpoche, came even closer to the ultimate reality when he said, "Nothing ever works out as you want, so give up all your schemes and ambitions. If you have to think about something, make it the uncertainty of the hour of your death."

Ben Johnson famously remarked that being hanged in the morning focuses the mind wonderfully. It is precisely this focus that Tibetan gurus attempt to instill in themselves and in their pupils. In a country where it is general practice to keep fires burning overnight, many Tibetan mystics permit theirs to go out . . . as a reminder that they might die in their sleep. They encourage their followers to embark on a meditation program based on the words of the Buddha:

> *Existence is as transient as autumn clouds. To watch the birth and death of beings is like looking at the movement of a dance. A lifetime is like a flash of lightning in the sky, rushing by like a torrent down a steep mountain.*

Although the meaning is clear enough, the masters realized that an intellectual understanding of impermanence is never enough to change a person's behavior, and without change nothing can be achieved. As long ago as the twelfth century AD, the mystic Drakpa Gyaltsen observed, "Human beings spend all their lives preparing, preparing, preparing . . . but meet the next life unprepared." Consequently, the meditation regime will typically include the vivid visualization of death images.

Readers intent on following the Tibetan Way might usefully follow suit. Make your relaxation and meditation preparations as before and follow your breathing until your mind is calm. Take the words of the Lord Buddha quoted above as your initial focus, attempting to analyze their meaning as clearly as possible.

Follow up the initial analysis by visualizing vivid images of death—cattle lined up at the entrance to a slaughterhouse, fish caught in a net or dangling on a hook at the end of an angler's line, a condemned prisoner seated in the electric chair while warders make the preparations to throw the switch.

Try to place yourself *within* these pictures. Imagine yourself as one of those cows, one of those fish, that condemned prisoner. Imagine the smell of blood in your nostrils, the atavistic fear you feel as the line moves forward. Imagine your desperation as you struggle to free yourself from the net and gasp the unfamiliar air. Imagine your absolute helplessness strapped in the chair with the metal cap placed on your shaven head and your mind filled with the certain knowledge that death—your death—is no more than moments away.

The fact that you are imagining yourself dying as someone or something else—a cow, a fish, a criminal—will distance you enough from the final moments to allow you to remain calm and contemplate the pain, terror, and emotion in a detached way. But the visualizations will help you grasp the universal inevitability of death, the absolute impossibility of avoiding it, and the brutal fact that death does not always arrive as we would like it to, but often comes with attendant horrors.

Complete the meditation by attempting to visualize your *own* death, as the person you are, not through the surrogate experience of an animal or some other fictional human being. Begin with the perfect death, seeing yourself lined with age, slipping gently away in a comfortable bed with the loving support of family and friends around you.

When you are familiar with that scenario, move on to the less pleasant, and perhaps more likely, possibilities for your death. You might, for example, join the hundreds of thousands of United States citizens who die of heart disease every year, or suffer a lethal—and often wholly unexpected—stroke. You may find yourself among the one in four who fall foul of cancer.

If you elect to visualize the heart attack, it will be useful to remember that while much heart disease has a history, the big one can sometimes hit without warning so that you experience a sudden, crushing chest pain possibly radiating into the neck, arm(s), and back. It doesn't go away. Medication doesn't help, nor does rest. You could still be in agony after an hour or more. To go with the pain, you'll probably have difficulty breathing. You'll sweat. You'll feel nauseated. Your blood pressure will drop. Your heart will race, although the beat may be irregular. You'll feel a deep sense of impending doom.

All these symptoms should, if you can bear it, become a part of your visualization, because all these symptoms are possibilities when it comes to your last minutes. This visualization, and others like it, are not designed to frighten you, but to simply help you face the two great truths of life: that you really *will* die; and that you have absolutely no way of knowing when or how.

It is an observable fact that most of those forced to face their own impending mortality (through bad medical news, for example) tend to go through a panic-stricken process of denial, anger, bargaining with God, and so on before a final stage of calm acceptance is reached. Unfortunately, calm acceptance all too often arrives so close to actual death itself that opportunities for a major lifestyle change are necessarily limited.

By using death-based meditation techniques, however, Tibetan mystics hope to reach the stage of calm acceptance in enough time to make their own preparations. What those preparations amount to is living well—not in the "eat, drink, and be merry" Western sense, but in the profound realization of what is actually important. You might, for example, find yourself far less concerned with wealth and far more concerned with people. You might come to value love over success, compassion over winning. You might wish to learn more, especially about yourself. Perhaps most important of all, you might like to devote a little time to something you have roundly ignored until now—inner preparations for the moment when your lu really is left behind to be embalmed, displayed, then buried and eventually forgotten in a cold, dark grave.

But that's just the lu. Any preparations you decide to make should, in the Tibetan view, be predicated on the certain knowledge that your job is far from over when you die.

CHAPTER TWENTY-TWO

THE DEATH PROCESS

Death is not an event—it's a process.

It is most likely to occur in the small hours of the morning when your body is at its lowest ebb. You will probably be asleep when it happens, and you may well stay asleep, but there is a chance you will wake up. If you do, you'll discover that your breathing has become shallow and labored. You may be aware of facial twitches and muscle spasms. You may hear a curious gurgling in the back of the throat, the famous "death-rattle." Next thing you know, your heart will have stopped.

In the old days, that used to be it. Any competent doctor would have pronounced you dead as a doornail. But nowadays it's widely recognized that a stopped heart can start again, sometimes spontaneously, sometimes as the result of medical intervention. Because of this, the medical profession has taken to speaking of death in terms of "irreversible cardiac arrest." But even where your cardiac arrest really is irreversible, the final moment of death is still a little way off.

Your body is essentially a support system for your brain, supplying it with all necessary nutrients via the blood. Once your heart stops, blood no longer circulates. This may put your brain in trouble, but it won't give up right away. For anything up to three minutes, it continues to function as it has always done, but after that the nerve cells of the cerebral cortex begin to die.

After seven or eight minutes, the damage is irreversible, although there's still some electrical activity in the brain stem, which can continue to function for a few minutes longer. But however tenaciously your brain stem clings to life, it will starve eventually. When that happens, you're now brain dead. Yet there is still quite complex activity in your body.

At the moment your heart ceases to beat, your pupils dilate, your muscles relax, and your whole body begins to cool. While you were alive, several interrelated control mechanisms kept your body temperature around 98.6°F (37°C). Without a heartbeat, those mechanisms cease to function. As a result, your body temperature drops until it reaches that of your surroundings. This loss of heat happens from the outside in, with core temperature dropping last. But having cooled, the body will start to warm up again if left too long.

At this stage, your kidneys and liver are still alive at the cellular level, and will stay alive for a good half hour. So, curiously enough, will your heart. You can remove the heart from a corpse thirty minutes after it has stopped beating and transplant it into a waiting patient with every hope the operation will be a success. The corneas of your eyes last even longer—they're still viable for anything up to twelve hours, as is your skin. Although your blood has ceased to move, its white cells are still swimming, mindlessly seeking to protect you against microbial invasion for the next six hours.

Not all remaining life signs are at this microscopic level. You can still get a knee-jerk reflex out of a corpse for up to twenty minutes after death. Muscles will contract under electrical stimulation for several hours, although there are changes going on that will put a stop to this eventually. With your blood no longer circulating, oxygen is unavailable to muscle cells, which compensate by using stored carbohydrate. But this produces lactic acid, which builds up in the muscle tissue and turns you stiff.

The stiffening process starts between one and six hours after death and begins at the jaw, progressing downward until you're locked up all the way to your feet in a process known as *rigor mortis*—the stiffness of death. The rigor lasts about thirty-six hours, gradually breaking down as enzymes eat the proteins that hold muscle fibers together.

Somewhere between half an hour and two hours after your heart stops, dark-colored spots start to show up on your skin, growing larger and more extensive over the next eight to twelve hours. The process is known as *livor mortis,* and comes about because gravity pools blood in various low-lying areas of your motionless body.

But neither rigor nor livor mortis are the worst of your problems. Since your immune system has now closed down, *Escherishia coli* bacteria begin to multiply in your intestine. Within two days they will spread enough to raise your body temperature. This is not, however, a sign of better health—decomposition has begun as the bacteria begin to eat their former home. In the process, they release such copious quantities of gas that the intestine eventually ruptures, allowing the bacteria to enter the blood and attack the other organs. The cadaver itself begins to swell and to smell.

How long it all takes depends on the ambient temperature. But given a week or two, your hair, fingernails, and teeth become detachable. After about a month, your tissues begin to liquefy. Initial putrefaction transforms into black putrefaction. At this stage your body begins to collapse in on itself and the smell is just about as bad as it's going to get.

By now your corpse is beginning to dry out, but some flesh remains and the smell turns cheesy. The skin cracks like old paint and mold begins to form on the abdominal surfaces. In a few more months, the cadaver dries out more or less completely. Decay continues slowly now. In time, there will be nothing left but bones.

But all that is just your body. The real mystery is what happens to your mind.

In the scientific West, this is scarcely a mystery at all. Without the support system of the body, the mind simply ceases: now you see it, now you don't. That inner entity you've always believed was you flickers out like a candle flame. But Tibetan mystics beg leave to disagree.

As noted earlier, Tibetan meditators were quick to conclude that the mind itself is not what we normally experience it to be. This went beyond their key concept of pure mind as the foundation of reality. They agreed with Western psychology that there are areas of the mind of which you are normally unaware, what various European and American schools of thought call the *subconscious, unconscious,* and *superconscious.* But they also postulated certain mind/energy interactions wholly unsuspected in the West.

As mentioned briefly earlier, in 1992 this point was taken up by the Dalai Lama himself when he spoke about mind-energy interdependence at the fourth biennial Mind and Life Conference in Dharamsala, India. He told a rapt audience that mind and consciousness could not be seen as separate, although both exhibited many subtle levels. It was, he said, the Tibetan belief that consciousness—at least the consciousness we experience in everyday life—is entirely dependent on the brain. This meant that once brain death occurred, the familiar experience of consciousness could no longer arise.

At this point, it seemed as if the Dalai Lama were siding with those in the West who maintain that death represents simple annihilation. But then he went on to say it was also the observation of Tibetan meditators that a subtle "essence of mind" existed independently of the brain and pervaded the body's energy system. This meant that from the Tibetan perspective, mind *could* survive brain death, at least for as long as the body's energy system remained functional.

But the Dalai Lama was being cautious in the face of an international audience. Tibetan mystics accept that an essence of mind survives even when the entire physical basis of the energy system has ceased to exist. They have developed a view of the death process as detailed as the one I have already given, but taken from a wholly different viewpoint. Where the West has concentrated on what happens to your body on the outside, Tibetan investigators tried to find out what happens on the inside, to your mind. What they discovered is, to say the least, intriguing.

According to their findings, the first symptom of death is weakness, followed by sinking and melting sensations. Your vision blurs, as if the world were under water. You begin to lose sensation. Your body numbs, sights and sounds fade. You are aware of growing cold and your consciousness begins to fade. Nothing seems to matter very much anymore. You experience a curious sense of calm. Smell, touch, and taste diminish, then disappear. Your breathing weakens and eventually stops.

This point exactly coincides with the Western concept of clinical death. Your heartbeat, blood flow, and electrical brain activity have all ceased. But, according to Tibetan findings, there is still activity, unsuspected by Western science, in the energy channels. Although your thoughts have dimmed and you have lost touch with the physical world, there is a dreamlike perception of luminous darkness before you undergo an experience very similar to passing out or falling asleep.

This, the Tibetans believe, is the real moment of death. Your mind has become so tenuous it is scarcely detectable, even to you. But then, after a moment of darkness, you become aware of what's going on around you—from a whole different perspective. You are no longer locked inside the aged body lying on the bed. You have emerged from it, stepped outside of it, and are, it must be said, feeling a great deal better than you did a moment ago. You can see what's happening, see the doctor who attended you, see the friends who have gathered around your deathbed. But it quickly becomes clear that they can't see you and they can't hear your reassurances that a miracle has happened, everything is all right, and you aren't dead after all. It doesn't feel like it, but it's as if you've suddenly become a ghost.

And you may *actually* become a ghost—the sort that haunts old houses and rattles chains. It doesn't happen often, but according to Tibetan research, it does happen sometimes. If you're the sort of person who's formed deep attachments to the material world, you could decide you really don't want to leave it. In such circumstances, you'll set off in your ghost body trying to contact people and influence events. If you're particularly stubborn, you will keep trying to influence events even when experience shows that you aren't succeeding very well. If your presence impinges on others—as it can do given the right combination of circumstances—a haunting results.

But mostly this doesn't happen. While your feelings will probably keep you hanging around for a while, the worst that's likely to occur is that you drift into the dreams of friends or relatives before passing beyond the physical world altogether.[88]

What comes next is fascinating.

---

88. As you may have realized from earlier chapters, Tibetan mystics view dreams as "objective" worlds rather than personal creations.

CHAPTER TWENTY-THREE

ADRIFT IN THE BARDOS

Extremely evil people—those whose lives were filled with fury—hurtle after death to be reborn at once in the hell realms. But such people are fortunately rare. According to Tibetan wisdom, the rest of us—good, bad, and indifferent—are destined to experience a sequence of post-mortem visions, vivid dreams that have a common structure for the whole of humanity.

Conventional Tibetan doctrine speaks of encountering the deities and demons of the bardo realms, but there is perhaps more to this than meets the eye. The term *bardo* carries the meaning of an in-between realm, a world that exists between this life and your next incarnation. There is no definition or description appended, no sense of reward, punishment, or waiting like in the heaven, hell, or purgatory of Christian theology. In fact, the bardos may not be worlds at all, but rather states of mind. In Buddhism it is often difficult to separate these things out, since ultimately all is mind in any case.

And whatever about the bardos, Tibetan mystics take a sophisticated view of the deities and demons, who are not thought of as entities in their own right, but rather embodiments of various facets of enlightenment inherent in your deepest mind. They are, in short, projections.

In Tibet, such projections would naturally take on Tibetan cultural guise. But you encounter what you expect, and your deep mind will seize on whatever religious imagery is most familiar to you. Thus, if you are Christian, you may meet up with Jesus and his saints, Satan and his devils. In neither case will you meet the real thing. You are, in a strange and wonderful sense, simply encountering yourself. But because your deep mind has the same basic structure as the rest of humanity whatever your cultural overlay, the sequence of visions will always be the same, as will the underlying energies and principles represented. Tibetans say that if you can somehow recognize them as such, your chance of liberation and enlightenment increases hugely.

So what happens as you finally withdraw from the physical world?

Everything is spelled out in a Tibetan text so remarkable in its content that it is now justly famous throughout the world. The text is called the *Bardo Thodol,* almost invariably translated as "The Tibetan Book of the Dead," although Tibetans themselves more often refer to the *Tibetan Book of the Great Liberation,* while the literal translation is simply "The Book of the Betweens."

According to this text, the visions really start as you begin to drift away from those who surround your deathbed. At this point, you will become aware of strange lights, bright colors, loud noise ("like the sound of a thousand crashes of thunder"). The experience can be frightening if you didn't expect it, but is, in fact, quite harmless and signifies only that you are approaching the spiritual planes. All phenomena at this stage are an expression of spiritual energies and should not be interrupted. By now you may begin to suspect you are dead,[89] which Tibetan mystics believe is a very good thing. They further suggest that you try to see connection with or separation from friends and relatives—two sides of the same coin—as a futile illusion, no longer relevant to your current state and best abandoned as soon as possible.

---

89. Something not at all obvious when it happens to you.

The *Bardo Thodol* mentions that since your mind has now been separated from your body, you no longer experience time as you did while in incarnation, but for the convenience of readers, it goes on to list the various visionary experiences on a day-to-day basis. Even as a convenience, this is *slightly* misleading, since there are indications that the actual time you devote to each experience depends largely on your spiritual state. Nonetheless, for the vast majority of us, this is what will happen following a four-and-a-half day period of unconsciousness:

Day 1

The visions of the first day are characterized by the appearance of a bright, deep, sky-blue light of great purity. From out of this light appears the deity Vairochana, the Illuminator, an inhabitant of the central Buddha-Realm Ghanavyuha, seated on a lion throne and holding an eight-spoked wheel. Vairochana is accompanied by his consort, the Lady of the Space Realm, whom he embraces fondly.[90]

Day 2

On the second day the blue radiance changes to a white light, associated by Tibetans with the element of water. As you experience this radiance, the deity Akshobbya—known to Tibetans as "Blessed"—appears before you, seated on an elephant throne and accompanied by an entourage of two bodhisattvas, Kshitigarbha and Maitreya, and two goddesses, Lasya and Pushpa. Akshobbya is blue in color and carries a vajra[91] while embracing his consort Buddha-lochana.

Day 3

By the third day, the color of the radiance has changed again, this time to a yellow light, which, for Tibetans, is associated with the earth

---

90. Some commentators assume that the embrace is sexual, symbolizing the interdependence of the twin aspects of enlightenment that these deities represent.

91. Another term for the ritual implement dorje, but one that carries philosophical overtones of adamantine wisdom.

element. Now the Blessed Ratnasambhava emerges from the southern realm of Shrimat to appear before you. He is yellow in color, seated on a horse throne, and carries a gemstone in one hand.[92] His entourage consists of the bodhisattvas Akashagarba and Samantabhadra, and the goddesses Mala and Dhupa. He embraces his consort Mamaki.

Day 4

At this stage, the color of the light changes to the red of the fire element, and the Blessed Amitabha emerges from the western realm of Sukhavati to appear before you. He is seated on a peacock throne, embracing his consort Pandaravasini while holding a lotus flower in his hand. Amitabha is red in color and accompanied by the bodhisattvas Avalokiteshvara and Manjushri, and the goddesses Gita and Aloka.

Day 5

On the fifth day, the green light of the air element—called "the wind element" in Tibet—begins to manifest, and you are confronted by the green-skinned deity Amoghasiddhi, who is seated on an eagle throne and carrying crossed vajras in one hand. Amoghasiddhi, who comes from the northern realm, embraces his consort Tara and is accompanied by the bodhisattvas Vajrapani and Sarvanivarana-vishkambhin, and the goddesses Gandha and Naivedya.

Day 6

At this point, your visionary experience becomes substantially more complex. The single purity of light that manifested during the previous days is replaced by a rainbow of white, yellow, red, and green elemental lights emerging from the four quarters.[93] It is as if you are observing a vast ritual field taking up the whole of space. Illuminated

---

92. This jewel is supposed to grant wishes, another intriguing piece of symbolism when set against the backdrop of Buddhist philosophy.

93. Readers familiar with the element/quarter associations of the Western Esoteric Tradition will by now have realized that these differ from the associations accepted in Tibet, as, of course, do some of the colors associated with the elements.

by the four lights, Vairochana and his consort, the Lady of the Space Realm, appear to take up the central position. Then, in the east, the Blessed Akshobbya and his consort Buddha-lochana emerge with their entourage. Next, Ratnasambhava and Mamaki appear in the south with their entourage. Now Amitabha and Pandaravasini lead their entourage in the west. Finally, green-skinned Amoghasiddhi and the beautiful Tara appear with their entourage in the north.

Once the Buddha-deities have taken their places, less familiar beings begin to appear. First come eight wrathful gatekeepers, stationed in male/female consort pairs at the four quarters: white Vijaya and his consort Ankusha in the east, yellow Yamantaka and his consort Pasha in the south, red Hayagriva and his consort Shrinkhala in the west, and green Amritakundali and his consort Ghanta in the north.

Now these entities are joined by six savior Buddhas: the black Dharmaraja associated with the salvation of the hell realms, the red Jvalamaraja of the hungry ghost realm, the blue Dhruvasimba of the animal realm, the yellow Shakyasimba of the human realm, the green Vemacitra of the demi-god realm, and the white Indra of the god realm. Finally, these Buddha figures are joined by two archetypal entities known in Tibet as Samantabhadra, the All-Good Father, and Samantabhadri, the All-Good Mother.

If you have been visualizing the events of Day 6, you will realize by now that what it being described is a colorful mandala structure of forty-two beings, similar in many respects to the *thangkas*[94] often found in Tibetan monasteries.

Day 7

The mandala format is maintained throughout this day as well, although it is a different mandala with different deities. Here the gods are known as *vidyadharas,* a term applied to a fully realized tantric master in the physical realm, but believed to manifest as an archetypal

---

94. Protective mandala paintings of the Buddha on silk, with embroidered silk surrounds.

aspect in the spiritual realm. In the center of a multicolored field of light, the supreme vidyadhara, the Lotus Lord of the Dance, appears with his red dakini consort. They dance together, faces turned to the sky, while wielding curved knives and holding blood-filled cups that appear to be formed from human skulls.

The mandala begins to form as the white, smiling deity named He Who Abides on the Levels appears in the east with his dakini consort. They, too, begin to dance, holding knives and blood-filled cups. Next, and similarly-equipped, He Who Has Mastery of Life appears smiling in the south, yellow in color and accompanied by his yellow dakini consort. Then, in the west, the Great Seal vidyadhara emerges, red in color and accompanied by his red dakini. Finally, in the north, the stern-faced, green vidyadhara named Spontaneous Accomplishment makes his appearance with his green dakini consort.

As the four cardinal *vidyadharas* dance with their consorts, wielding their knives and skull-cups, they are gradually surrounded by a vast host of dakinis and protectors of religion, rather worryingly wearing bone ornaments and carrying banners, ribbons, and pennants made from human skin. Many of them play *kanglings* (human thighbone trumpets) and drums made from human skulls. There is a smell of singed human flesh, burned like incense.

Day 8

Day 7, as you may have realized from the symbolism, marks a turning point of sorts in your death process. The Tibetans group post-mortem visions into two broad categories: those typified by the appearance of peaceful deities and those in which the deities are wrathful. Day 7 marks the gradual transformation from one to the other, but by Day 8, the transformation is complete and the deities who appear from now on are quite definitely wrathful.

The horror begins with the emergence (from the middle of your head) of the fearful Buddha Heruka, a three-headed creature, maroon in color, with six arms and four legs. Each of the three faces of this creature—colored white, red, and maroon, respectively—has three eyes. He wears a crown of skulls and adorns his body with black snakes and a string of newly severed human heads.

Buddha Heruka stands on a throne held up by enormous eaglelike birds. With him, wrapped around him, is his equally fearsome consort Buddha-Krodheshvari, who feeds him from a skull-cup brimming with blood. Both deities glare and roar at you as their bodies emit huge bursts of flame.

Day 9

On this day, the dreaded Vajra Heruka appears from the east, entwined around his consort Vajra-Krodheshvari, who feeds him blood from a skull-cup. Vajra Heruka, like his predecessor of the previous day, has three heads, four legs, and six arms. His faces are red, white, and dark blue in color. In one hand he holds a vajra, in another a skull-cup, in another an axe, in another a bell, in another a plowshare, and in his sixth hand a second skull-cup.

Day 10

Now there appears from the south a third wrathful deity, Ratna Heruka, and his consort Ratna-Krodheshvari. Cast in the same six-armed/four-legged/three-headed mold as before, Ratna Heruka has a dark yellow body and three faces, yellow, white, and red. He holds a jewel, a spear (gruesomely impaling three heads), a club, a bell, a skull-cup, and a trident. Like the others, he is being fed blood by his consort.

Day 11

By this point, Ratna Heruka is replaced by Padma Heruka from the west, entwined about by his consort Padma-Krodheshvari, who again feeds him blood from a skull-cup. His three faces are white, red, and dark red. In his six hands he carries a lotus, a spear with three impaled heads, a staff, a bell, a small drum, and, like his wife, a blood-filled skull-cup.

Day 12

On Day 12, you will be confronted by yet another variation on the basic theme, the wrathful deity Karma Heruka and his blood-feeding consort Karma-Krodheshvari. The deity's body is dark green in color and his faces are white, red, and green, respectively. He holds a sword, a spear with three impaled heads, a staff, a bell, a skull-cup, and a plowshare.

Day 12 marks the end of the formalized day-to-day visions, but your troubles aren't over yet. Almost as a crescendo to the whole of the after-death experience, you are likely to meet up with entities the Tibetans call the Eight Maidens, the Eight Witches, the Four Gatekeepers, the Twenty-Eight Ladies, and the Lords of Death.

Eight Maidens

Despite their sweet name, the Eight Maidens are, in fact, frenzied female horrors with much in common with the Harpies of Greek mythology. They appear one by one from the eight directions (east, south, west, north, southeast, southwest, northwest, northeast) to surround the five blood-drinking Herukas.

From the east, a white Maiden appears, wielding a corpse like a club and carrying a blood-filled skull-cup.

From the south, a yellow Maiden appears, holding a drawn bow.

From the west, a red Maiden appears, holding a crocodile-skin banner.

From the north, a black Maiden appears, carrying a vajra and a blood-filled skull-cup.

From the southeast, an orange Maiden appears. She feeds on a coil of human intestines.

From the southwest, a dark-green Maiden appears, drinking blood from a skull-cup and carrying a vajra.

From the northwest, a pale-yellow Maiden appears, chewing on a corpse while holding its ripped-out heart in one hand.

From the northeast, a dark-blue Maiden appears. She, too, is a corpse-eater, having ripped her victim's head from his body.

Eight Witches

Hard on the heels of the Eight Maidens come the Eight Witches, even more bestial and repulsive women who also surround the Herukas.

From the east appears a dark-maroon, lion-headed Witch, nonchalantly chewing on a corpse.

From the south appears a red, tiger-headed Witch, glaring and snarling.

From the west appears a black, fox-headed Witch, carrying a razor and feeding off blood-soaked human intestines.

From the north appears a dark-blue, wolf-headed Witch with glaring eyes, who also feeds on a human corpse.

From the southeast appears a pale-yellow, vulture-headed Witch, carrying a corpse over one shoulder and holding a skeleton in her hands.

From the southwest appears a dark-red, vulture-headed Witch, wearing a flayed human skin like a shawl.

From the northwest appears a black, crow-headed Witch, holding a blood-filled skull-cup in one hand and a sword in the other while she gnaws enthusiastically on a human heart and lungs.

From the northeast appears a dark-blue, owl-headed Witch, who holds a sword in one hand and a vajra in the other.

Four Gatekeepers

By now it is clear that you are witnessing the creation of a terrifying living mandala, and at this point four impressive female guardians appear at its inner gates, taking up positions at the cardinal points.

First, from the east comes a white, horse-headed Gatekeeper, holding an iron crook and blood-filled skull-cup.

Next, from the south comes a yellow, pig-headed Gatekeeper, holding a noose.

Next, from the west comes a red, lion-headed Gatekeeper, holding an iron chain.

Finally, from the north comes a green, serpent-headed Gatekeeper, holding a bell.

Twenty-Eight Ladies

To complete the massive mandala, twenty-eight animal-headed Ladies appear in groups of six and four. As with the Gatekeepers, Witches, and Maidens, these entities appear in the form of creatures from Tibetan (and often Indian) mythology.

From the east will emerge six Ladies: one dark-maroon, yak-headed, holding a vajra; one orange, serpent-headed, holding a lotus; one dark-green, leopard-headed, holding a trident; one blue, mongoose-headed, holding a wheel; one red, bear-headed, holding a spear; and one white, bear-headed, holding a noose of intestines.

These are followed by six Ladies emerging from the south: one yellow, sow-headed, holding a razor; one red, crocodile-headed, holding a jar; one red, scorpion-headed, holding a lotus; one white, hawk-headed, holding a vajra; one dark-green, fox-headed, holding a club; one dark-yellow, tiger-headed, holding a skull-cup of blood.

Then come six Ladies from the west: one dark-green, vulture-headed, holding a club; one red, horse-headed, holding a human torso; one white, eagle-headed, holding a club; one red, dog-headed, holding a vajra razor; one red, hoopoe-headed, drawing a bow; one dark-green, deer-headed, holding a jar.

Next come six Ladies from the north: one blue, wolf-headed, holding a banner; one red, ibex-headed, holding a stake; one black, sow-headed, holding a noose; one red, crow-headed, holding the flayed skin of a child; one dark-green, elephant-headed, holding a human corpse; one blue, serpent-headed, holding a snake-noose.

Finally, four more Ladies emerge to form the outer gatekeepers of the mandala.

From the east comes a white, cuckoo-headed Lady, holding an iron crook.

From the south comes a yellow, goat-headed Lady, holding a noose.

From the west comes a red, lion-headed Lady, holding an iron chain.

From the north comes a green, serpent-headed Lady, holding a bell.

Lords of Death

Finally, to complete this universe of horrors, every figure in your field of vision transforms into a Lord of Death. You will also become aware that the entire universe is now filled with the Lords of Death, enormous, gibbering demons who tear bodies apart and suck out their brains, who rip out hearts and intestines as they hurl threats at you.

Not unexpectedly, the sheer horror of this ghastly experience will cause you to faint in terror. The last you will remember of the bardos is the welcoming embrace of dark unconsciousness.

CHAPTER TWENTY-FOUR

REBIRTH

You will come to eventually, of course. How long you fainted is irrelevant: we have already noted that the familiar experience of sequential time no longer holds good in the post-mortem state. What *is* important is that the demons are gone. All those threatening, blood-drinking entities have vanished completely. And something else has changed as well. Your mind is clearer, your thoughts more lucid. As you look around, you will discover, probably with delight, that you are back in the real, physical world.

What's more, you seem to have been given your old body back.

For a moment you may even suspect that you never really died at all. Perhaps it was all a near-death experience, complete with vivid hallucinations of deities and demons. But as you approach your old home and meet up with your surviving relatives and friends, you will quickly come to realize that the body you occupy, while it feels perfectly solid, is actually the body of a ghost. You can easily walk through walls, and when you try to speak to your loved ones, it is quite clear they do not hear you. However much you cling to them, however much you shout at them, they will ignore you.

This, as much as anything else, will convince you that you must have died and are now occupying some sort of astral body. Already, memories of your bardo experiences are fading, as if they were little more than a dream. But this is reality: you have died and become a ghost. The realization causes a curious change in your environment. At the edges of your vision there is a murky haze, gray and gloomy, as if you were surrounded by an encroaching fog.

For about twenty-one days[95] you are condemned to wander the earth in this state. But not happily. Something in you seems to be attracted by natural disasters—fires, floods, hurricanes, avalanches, and the like—and while experience shows that nothing can harm your new body, you still feel under threat, as if pursued by demons.

Although your astral body looks and feels solid enough to you, the reality is that you are a disembodied mind. While you are back *in* the world, you are no longer *of* the world, and lacking a physical anchor will leave you nervous and restless. You are likely to be assailed by phantom sensations of cold or pain. You will be pray to emotions like despondency and anger. A part of you may even feel as if you are growing unhinged.

But the overriding factor is the knowledge that you are dead and alone—and have not the slightest idea what to do next.

In desperation, you may even seek out your old body—if it hasn't yet been buried, rotted, or cremated—and try to re-enter it. But you will not succeed. The plain truth is your old body has become a corpse and the dead do not rise again. You will begin an anxious search for a living body to take over.

There is substantial evidence that the phenomenon of spirit possession is a literal reality, and if so, it seems most likely to arise at this stage of the death process. But actual possession is, fortunately, rare—occupied bodies seem to be naturally well-defended—so that even if your own morality does not stop you from trying to evict a tenant, the chances are hugely against your being able to do so.

---

95. An approximation and perhaps an average. The actual time period is determined by your karma.

Without a body, the bardo visions may arise again, but nowhere so structured and formalized as they were before. Instead, as a Tibetan with a firm belief in karma—or even as a Westerner with a belief in sin—you may become aware of the Lord of Death standing judgment over you. Your past misdeeds will be shown to you in such vivid detail that you must realize that all of your old attempts to lie and cover up have come to nothing. The Lord of Death, having found you very wanting, will seize you, place a rope around your neck, and dismember you, time and again.

But this penalty, while clearly terrifying, is more symbolic than actual, since your astral body is impervious to physical harm. The Lord of Death will eventually release you to your empty wanderings, themselves more bleak than any punishment that could have been imposed.

By now you are desperate for a new (physical) body, and even more desperate for a change—any change—in your current circumstances. Novelty of any sort will attract you like a magnet.

And at some stage, something new and exciting *will* arise: the appearance of six lights—one a soft white, one red, one blue, one green, one yellow, and one a smoky gray. You may not realize it at the time, but these are the lights of the Six Realms of Buddhist doctrine—white for the god realm, red for the demi-god realm, blue for the human realm, green for the animal realm, yellow for the hungry ghost realm, and gray for the hell realms. One light will shine brighter than all the rest, and you will be hugely attracted to it. Soon you will notice that your astral body has taken on the same coloring as this light. You will begin to move toward it.

Whichever of the realms you enter, you will find yourself drawn toward couples engaged in sexual intercourse, possibly impelled by memories of the most pleasurable drive you experienced in your last incarnation. At the same time, you may have visionary flashes of various places and situations into which you might be reborn. Some of these will attract you more than others. Your fascination with the act of lovemaking will increase. You will, perhaps, move closer to get a better look.

Then, as conception occurs, you will find yourself sucked into the womb to mingle with the cells of a newly evolving body.

And there you will stay for a nine-month period, patiently awaiting the daylight of your next incarnation.

CHAPTER TWENTY-FIVE

LIBERATION

Or perhaps not. I have been a little less than honest with you in the last three chapters, or at least a little less than complete. The *Bardo Thodol* is not simply a description of the rebirth process, but an instruction manual on how to avoid it. For Tibetan mystics, the ultimate goal is liberation from samsara, escape from the eternal wheel of birth, death, and rebirth that continuously locks us into the world of suffering and pain. Thus, in Tibet, the whole of the *Bardo Thodol* is read aloud to the faithful as they approach the point of death and to their corpse for several days thereafter in the hope of guiding the spirit to liberation or, if all else fails, a favorable rebirth.

The timing is perfect. Tibetan mystics wholly support the Buddhist doctrine of nonattachment, and what better time to detach from worldly concerns than when you are dead? It is difficult to work up much enthusiasm for the office when your heart has stopped and your brain has flatlined. Furthermore, there is a very special opportunity for liberation that presents itself to everyone, *whatever their religious belief or level of spiritual evolution,* immediately after death occurs. If you can recognize and seize it, you're home free.

To examine this unique moment, we need to return to the death process as described earlier. You may recall that I wrote of the precise instant of death in the following terms:

*Your mind has become so tenuous it is scarcely detectable,
even to yourself. But then, after a moment of darkness, you
become aware of what's going on around you . . . from a
whole different perspective. You are no longer locked inside
the aged body lying on the bed.*

The important phrase here is "moment of darkness," which, while
accurate so far as it goes, is essentially misleading. This instant
appears, *in retrospect*, to be the darkness of a swoon, a brief moment
of unconsciousness occasioned by a faint. But only in retrospect. It is,
in fact, something far closer to a moment of amnesia. What really
happens, according to Tibetan mystical doctrine, is this:

As physical processes cease and the senses dim, consciousness
itself begins to weaken. At the same time, important—and terminal—
changes are taking place in your subtle energy system. The energies
that normally reside in the upper halves of your left and right rtsa
channels flow upward to merge at the crown of your head and enter
the central channel.

This new influx of energy dislodges a white beadlike drop of subtle essence donated by your father at the time of your conception. As
the drop is pushed down the midline channel, you will experience a
vision of whiteness, similar to bright moonlight.

While this is going on, the energies in the lower halves of the rtsa
channels are also merging, this time at the base of your spine. They
too enter the central channel, where they begin to push upward a red
beadlike drop of energy that was donated by your mother at the time
of your conception. The movement causes the subjective impression
of a red light, somewhat brighter than the white light you are already
experiencing.

The downward movement of the upper energies and the upward
movement of the lower continue until the two beads meet about the
level of the heart and all energetic activity then ceases. At this
moment, the "moment of darkness" in our earlier description, you
will find yourself experiencing a bright, empty, radiant light, devoid of

any other characteristics, yet somehow encompassing all and everything there is. Physical death has stripped away all psychic structures, leaving only the fundamental bedrock of mind, on which all experience is built. You are, so to speak, staring into what Tibetans call the Clear Light. All you need to do now is allow the remnants of your consciousness to merge with it and you will have achieved your full and final liberation.

Unfortunately, most of us never recognize the Clear Light for what it is. It appears only as a huge, blinding, terrifying glare. Lacking the spiritual knowledge and discipline to seize the moment,[96] we panic, and, in the words of the *Bardo Thodol*, flee from the light.

But this is no simple flight. To protect yourself from the horror of naked existence, you begin, quite automatically and instinctively, to rebuild those inner structures that enabled you to experience the phenomenal world you so recently left. Among those structures is an energy body—possibly an electrical field with an attached node of consciousness—that permits you to reawaken by your deathbed. The brief moment of possibility has passed. Your memory contains only an instant of blankness. It *feels* as if a ghost has emerged from your physical body at the point of death, but this is an illusion. Your original "ghost" (astral energy body) broke down soon after the death of the physical, but since you were not able to endure the primal existence of pure enlightenment, you built yourself another one, and it is the new ghost that you inhabit now.

What happens to you next is largely illusory as well. The deities and demons of the bardos certainly are. Your new energy body is, in these early stages, weak and incomplete. It enables you to escape the terror of pure mind and experience, to some degree, the world you left behind. But it is not functioning fully. Your consciousness is fluid and cannot altogether maintain the familiar samsaric structures. You drift like someone who is half caught inside a dream, an experience you are

---

96. And it tends to be, according to Tibetan doctrine, a very fleeting moment indeed.

likely to interpret (perhaps more correctly than we realize) as moving toward the spiritual realms.

You are in fact drifting back toward the Clear Light of your primordial mind. But the mental and energetic structures you have now created—albeit weakly—mean you no longer experience it with the purity you did at the moment of your death. Now you permit it to manifest only in symbols, projections of its own essence, modified by the psychic structures you are currently creating. The bardos may seem absolutely real to you, but they are actually dreams. The entities who emerge within them are all, without exception, creations of your own deep mind.

This is why so much of the bardo experience takes on the appearance of a mandala. Carl Jung discovered, while still very much alive, that the mandalas drawn by his patients were aspirational portraits of an unfragmented mind. Your post-mortem experience of that mind—totality emerges, on the bardos, using exactly the same symbolism.

At first, the projections are benign, as befits the mystical experience of Ultimate Reality. But even as you pass from day to day, bardo to bardo, you continue to build your inner protections so that the projections of the deep mind become increasingly distorted until your perceptions are filled by the paranoid delusion of a malignant universe jam-packed with destructive demons.

At any point along the process, as the whispered instructions of the *Bardo Thodol* will inform you, you can escape from the dreams and nightmares *by recognizing them for what they are,* projections of your own psychic processes, and by accepting the Clear Light that lies beneath.

But without spiritual preparation and insight, that acceptance becomes increasingly difficult the longer you leave it.

During the final stages of your dream encounters, your consciousness is moving further from its essence as the subtle body you are building grows stronger. Your thoughts turn toward the familiar reassurances of physical existence, and your memories generate desire, which draws you back to the world of matter.

Many Tibetans believe that while your karma determines the world in which you are destined to be reborn, it is your fantasies of sexual pleasure that bring you into the proximity of couples who are making love. When your spirit drifts too close to an act of conception, it is drawn into the womb to begin your next life.

The electrical field "body," with its attached node of consciousness, contributes to the cellular programming that permits the new fetus to develop. Although the field contains memory imprints from your previous existence, these are not readily accessible to consciousness, which, in any case, changes its nature as the physical brain develops. The traces of some high-level traumas or persistent peculiarities can be passed on to the new body, but by the time you are born any memory of earlier existences will typically have disappeared.

You are ready to begin your next life with a clean slate.

CHAPTER TWENTY-SIX

DREAMING OF DEATH

Through the lucidity techniques of dream yoga, you can feel for your-self what it is like to slip into the Clear Light, then go on to interact with accurate mock-ups of the various bardo states that may arise. In this way, you train yourself to meet death in full consciousness of what is going on.

For practitioners of dream yoga, this training is an all-win situa-tion, whatever their individual state of spiritual evolution. If your spiritual practice has brought you close to enlightenment, the training will allow you to pass without fear or revulsion directly into the Clear Light state when you die—and stay there. You will bypass the experi-ence of the bardos. No longer will you need to reincarnate. Liberation and nirvana will be yours.

Less evolved individuals still retain the possibility of enlighten-ment as well. Even if you are unable to hold yourself in the Clear Light state at first, your lucid dream rehearsals will at least enable you to recognize it—and to predict the immanent appearance of the illusory bardos. This realization in itself can be enough to permit you resi-dence in the Clear Light, despite the small initial hiccup.

Since it is largely fear that drives people out of the Clear Light, even beginners can benefit from their experience with dream yoga. It allows them to understand that in the dreamlike death state there is nothing to fear and the "refuge" of reincarnation is an empty illusion. Sometimes that in itself can be enough to block the process of rebirth and allow the individual, with a little grit and determination, to seek out the realms of the Clear Light.

EPILOGUE

At least one scholar[97] has pointed out that there are two Tibets: the geographical reality on its Himalayan plateau and the Tibet of the Western imagination.

Both are extraordinarily interesting, but the second has seldom been consciously examined, let alone compared directly with the first. To the Western mind, Tibet is (or at least was) a land of mystery and marvels, a *Shangri-La* that, in the immortal words of Louis Armstrong, is "*really* la." We see it as a haven of spirituality, populated by smiling, peaceful people whose dedication to their religion might be an object lesson to us all.

We seldom think of Tibetans suffering from famine, like their unfortunate cousins in Africa. We never think of Tibetans planning to invade their neighbors, like some regimes of the Middle East. The idea of a corrupt Tibetan is beyond consideration. Tibet is Utopia. Tibet was paradise—at least until the miserable Chinese came along.

Like so many imaginary constructs, the Western view of Tibet is an intriguing mix of fact and fiction. It is certainly true that Tibet became one of the most religious countries on the face of the planet. It evolved an economy that was virtually a support system for its monasteries. Fully 25 percent of the population were monks or nuns, entirely sustained by the labor of the remaining 75 percent.

Tibetan religion was not a front for the sort of ecclesiastical power structure, so prevalent throughout the remainder of the world, that dedicates its efforts to the accumulation of wealth and the expansion

---

97. Peter Bishop, vide his book *Dreams of Power* (London: Athlone Press, 1993).

of political influence. There was a genuine interest in spirituality, the selfsame interest that created techniques of personal evolution like those outlined in this book.

But none of that made Tibet a Utopia. As we have already seen, the peaceful people of Tibet were once the most feared warriors in Asia. And even after the emergency of Buddhism, the horsemen of the Khampa region remained far more noted for their ferocity than for their meditation skills. Worse still, the administration of Tibet eventually fell foul to corruption and stagnation—the judgment is that of the present Dalai Lama—and was in need of urgent modernization and reform.

Against this paradoxical background, it becomes possible to make some sort of sense of developments from the midtwentieth century onward. Until the Chinese invasion, Tibet had been closed off for centuries. In an age of near-universal tourism, it remained *terra incognita*. Only a handful of foreigners were permitted to go in; only a few hundred Tibetans ever cared to go out.

As a result, the vast reservoir of Tibetan spirituality was confined to a single nation. Almost none of it leaked out to nourish the remainder of the world.

The Chinese invasion, brutal though it was, bloody though it was, unjustified though it was, immoral though it was, still managed, in that curious way in which spirit sometimes moves, to serve the cause of enlightenment. Once it became obvious that Maoist China had scant respect for Tibetan spirituality, Tibetan spirituality, for the first time in five hundred years, moved outside Tibet.

For the rest of the world, this was a development beyond price. Today, there are Tibetan religious communities scattered across almost every continent. (There is one less than a day's drive from where I write in Ireland.) Each is dedicated to preserving *and sharing* the fruits of Tibetan spirituality. And if there is none near you, this scarcely matters, for the great Tibetan spiritual texts, once the world's best-kept secrets, are now available from Amazon. In paperback.

This, quite simply, is benevolent karma in action. Hopefully the current book may persuade you to take advantage of it.

APPENDIX: TIBETAN LANGUAGE
AND PRONUNCIATION

To talk about a Tibetan language—as if there were only one—is something of a mistake. When the Chinese invaded in 1950, they discovered that the tongue spoken in the monasteries sounded very different from that of the common people. There was a third language spoken only at Court, full of honorifics denoting rank and respect. Wide gaps seemed to have sprung up between written Tibetan, which was clearly a religious language, and spoken Tibetan, which often concentrated on more mundane concerns.

To make matters worse, there were regional differences in pronunciation. Given that the written form reflected the pronunciation current when it was first introduced in the seventh century AD, the dialects of Western Tibet and Kham (to the East) seemed closest to the source, while Central Tibet and the capital Lhasa showed a whole range of modifications.

To compound their difficulties, they discovered a bewildering lack of generics. The Tibetans could, for example, speak of a poplar, spruce, or willow, yet lacked any word for the all-embracing term "tree."

Clearly, something had to be done. The Chinese set themselves the task of establishing "Standard Tibetan," based on the language of Lhasa. More than twenty years later, it was admitted that progress had proven "slow," although the invaders were optimistic that their approved forms would "eventually" spread throughout the population.

If the Chinese face problems, so too do Western scholars. Tibetan and English do not share a common alphabet so that all English renderings of Tibetan terms are necessarily approximate. Because of this—and, indeed, the pronunciation differences across Tibet itself—there can be considerable variations in transliteration. For example, renderings like *Lying* and *Ling* both point toward the same Tibetan original.

I have tried to keep transliterations in the present book as simple as possible, but even so there are likely to be pitfalls. The following (very) rough guide to the pronunciation of Tibetan terms may help readers avoid the worst of them.

The form *th* is not normally pronounced as a single sound. (As it is in such common English words as *three, though, throw,* and so on.) Instead, it is broken into its component sounds of *t* and *h,* as in "hot-**h**ouse." The same holds good for the usages *ph, dh, kh,* and *jh.*

The letter *c* generally sounds like *ch,* as in "child." The form *ch* follows the usage outlined in the last paragraph and is split into its components so that it sounds as *ch-h,* as in "mat**ch-h**ead." The letter *j* is equivalent to the English *j,* as in "**j**oke."

Some common and highly specific Tibetan transliterations are *ts* pronounced, as in "sigh**ts**"; *tsh,* which splits into the *ts* sound followed by *h,* as in "**h**all"; *z* is usually pronounced as in "**z**ero," but can sound as the *j* in French—that is, "bon-**j**our." (Some transliteration systems accent the letter to differentiate.)

Where Tibetan transliterations begin with groups of two or three consonants—like *gsang* ("secret") or *hkhor-lo* ("wheel")—the letters *b, d, g, h, l, m,* and *s* are silent. Of these, *d, l,* and *s* are also silent when they appear as a final consonant, although they tend to modify preceding vowels, except for *i* and *e.*

Finally, adding *y* to *b, m, p,* or *ph* modifies their pronunciation. The usage *by* is equivalent to *j; my* becomes *ny,* as in "can**y**on"; *py* is sounded *ch,* as in "**ch**urch"; while *phy* splits into *ch* and *h,* sounded as in "chur**ch-h**all."

GLOSSARY OF TIBETAN TERMS

Angkur: Empowerment in a particular ability, usually as passed from teacher to pupil.

Asura: Denizen of the demi-god realm.

Baian-Kara-Ula: A Tibetan mountain range.

Bardo Thodol: The Tibetan Book of the Dead.

Bardo: Strictly a state of consciousness, but most often used to describe one of the between-lives states experienced by the individual after death.

Bön: Aboriginal religion of Tibet.

Bönpoba: Practitioner of Bön.

Buddha: Enlightened one. Usually refers to the last historical Buddha, Prince Gautama of India.

Chang Thang: A region of Northern Tibet.

Chang: Ritual bell.

Chenresig: Patron god of Tibet, believed to incarnate as the Dalai Lama.

Chöd: A rite of magical self-acrifice.

Chöjung: Tibetan historical writings recorded in the thirteenth century.

Dakini: A female spirit being.

Dalai Lama: Secular and religious leader of Tibet.

Damaru: Small double drum.

Dbu-ma: Central energy channel of the human body.

Dorje Posture: Lotus posture of Hatha Yoga.

Dorje: Ritual implement. Also sometimes used to denote the "diamond body" that represents the individual's Buddha nature or divine spark.

Dunkong Shakgyapa: Early Buddhist scriptures.

Dzambu Lying: Planet Earth.

Dzopa: Tibetan hill tribe who believe themselves to be the descendants of space-faring aliens.

Gomchen: Mystic title translating as "great hermit."

Ham: Letter of the Tibetan alphabet.

Hdab-ston: Crown chakra.

Hum: Tibetan symbol for divine life force.

Hung: Tibetan syllable.

Jigten Chagtsul: Tibetan scriptures.

Kanchenjunga: World's second highest mountain.

Kangling: Human thighbone trumpet.

Kargyut-pa: School of Tibetan Buddhism founded by the Tibetan saint Marpa.

Khor ba: Suffering; equivalent to Indian term *sangsara*.

Khor-lo: Energy center (chakra) of the human body.

Kylkhor: Magic circle.

La: Tibetan syllable.

Lama: Tibetan monk.

Lha: Alien race that evolved into humanity.

Lhasa: The Tibetan capital.

Lung-gom-pa: Tibetan trance runner.

Maheketang: Ceremonial runner who chases demons.

Mala: Tibetan rosary.

Mandala: Balanced design motif used in meditation.

Nirvana: State achieved when the individual resolves all dualities and ceases to incarnate.

Om: Mantric sound supposed to reflect the keynote of the universe.

Panchen Lama: Second most senior lama of Tibet, next to the Dalai Lama.

Phag Ri: World's highest town.

Phurba: Ceremonial dart.

Pustaka: Small ceremonial image of a sacred book.

Ra: Tibetan syllable.

Repa: Light cotton robe. Also, by derivation, the title given to a tumo adept.

Rigpa: The experience of nonduality.

Rinpoche: Mystic title translating as "precious one."

Rirab Lhunpo: Home planet of the *Lha*.

Rkyang-ma: Left-hand energy channel of the human body.

Rlung: The energy that runs through the rtsa channels; equivalent to the ch'i of Chinese acupuncture.

Ro-ma: Right-hand energy channel of the human body.

Rtsa: Energy channel of the human body.

Sa: Tibetan syllable.

Samadhi: Ecstatic trance state often believed to be a prelude to nirvana.

Sang-na: Root chakra.

Sankha: Cermonial conch shell, used as a musical instrument.

Sha: Tibetan syllable.

Shalu Gompa: Tibetan monastery specializing in lung-gom-pa training.

Shugs: The energy contained in semen.

Thangka: Protective painting of the Buddha.

Thig-li: Subtle essences pervading each human being.

Tingshaw: Ceremonial cymbal.

Trisula: Ceremonial trident.

Tulpa: Thought-form entity.

Tumo: A form of yoga characterized by the generation of body heat.

Vajra-Yogini: Tantric goddess.

Yidam: Tutelary deity.

Zhiné: Contemplative meditation.

BIBLIOGRAPHY

Bishop, Peter. *Dreams of Power.* London: Athlone Press, 1993.

Blofeld, John. *The Tantric Mysticism of Tibet.* New York: E. P. Dutton & Co. Inc., 1970.

Brennan, J. H. *Discover Reincarnation.* London: Aquarian Press, 1992.

Butler, W. E. *The Magician: His Training and Work.* London: Aquarian Press, 1963.

Clifford, Terry. *Tibetan Buddhist Medicine and Psychiatry.* Maine: Samuel Weiser Inc., 1990.

David-Neel, Alexandra. *Initiations and Initiates in Tibet.* London: Rider, 1970.

———. *Magic and Mystery in Tibet.* London: Souvenir Press, 1967.

David-Neel, Alexandra, and Lama Yongden. *The Secret Oral Teachings in Tibetan Buddhist Sects.* San Francisco: City Lights, 1971.

Evans-Wentz, W. Y., ed. *Tibetan Yoga and Secret Doctrines* Oxford: Oxford University Press, 1969.

Ford, Robert. *Captured in Tibet.* London: Pan Books, 1958.

Govinda, Lama Anagarika. *Foundations of Tibetan Mysticism.* Maine: Samuel Weiser Inc., 1969.

Guiley, Rosemary Ellen. *Harper's Encyclopedia of Mystical and Paranormal Experience.* San Francisco: HarperSanFrancisco, 1991.

Gyatso, Geshe Kelsang. *A Meditation Handbook.* London: Tharpa Publications, 1993.

Hodge, Stephen, and Boord Martin. *The Illustrated Tibetan Book of the Dead.* New Alresford, Hants, England: Godsfield Press, 2000.

Houston, Jean. *The Hero and the Goddess.* London: Aquarian Press, 1993.

Jansen, Eva Rudy. *Singing Bowls.* Holland: Binkey Kok Publications, 1997.

Kelder, Peter. *Tibetan Secrets of Youth and Vitality.* Wellingborough: Aquarian Press, 1988.

Landon, Perceval. *Lhasa.* Published in two vols. London: Hurst and Blackett, 1905.

Rinpoche, Sogyal. *The Tibetan Book of Living and Dying.* London: Rider, 1992.

Snellgrove, David L., and Hugh Richardson. *A Cultural History of Tibet.* Bancock: Orchid Press, 2003.

Thurman, Robert A. F. *Essential Tibetan Buddhism.* New Jersey: Castle Books, 1995.

———. *The Tibetan Book of the Dead.* London: Aquarian Press, 1994.

Yeshe, Lama, and Zopa Rinpoche. *Wisdom Energy.* Boston: Wisdom Publications, 2000.